湖南省教学改革研究项目《数字化赋能高职公共英语课程
境及破解路径研究》（项目编号：ZJGB2023685）的阶段性研究成果

谢丹　著

数字化赋能
高职公共英语金课建设

Construction of High-quality
Vocational College English Courses
Empowered by Digitalization

西南交通大学出版社
·成　都·

图书在版编目（CIP）数据

数字化赋能高职公共英语金课建设 / 谢丹著.
成都：西南交通大学出版社，2025. 3. -- ISBN 978-7
-5774-0384-7

Ⅰ. H319.3-39

中国国家版本馆 CIP 数据核字第 2025SB7404 号

Shuzihua Funeng Gaozhi Gonggong Yingyu Jinke Jianshe

数字化赋能高职公共英语金课建设

谢 丹 著

策 划 编 辑	郭发仔
责 任 编 辑	孟 媛
责 任 校 对	左凌涛
封 面 设 计	墨创文化
出 版 发 行	西南交通大学出版社
	（四川省成都市金牛区二环路北一段 111 号
	西南交通大学创新大厦 21 楼）
营 销 部 电 话	028-87600564　028-87600533
邮 政 编 码	610031
网 址	https://www.xnjdcbs.com
印 刷	成都蜀通印务有限责任公司
成 品 尺 寸	170 mm × 230 mm
印 张	9
字 数	215 千
版 次	2025 年 3 月第 1 版
印 次	2025 年 3 月第 1 次
书 号	ISBN 978-7-5774-0384-7
定 价	49.00 元

Preface

Vocational college English courses, as compulsory courses or restricted elective courses for higher vocational college students of non-English majors, plays an important role in fostering the students' practical English-language competence, cultural awareness and intercultural communication skills. They promote the students' cognitive development in language learning, thereby better cultivate students' thinking and self-expression abilities. They are also beneficial for forging the students' global mindset, broadening their international horizons, enhancing their pride and confidence in Chinese culture, and developing the correct outlook on the world, on life and on values.

Digitalization refers to enabling or improving processes by leveraging digital technologies represented by cloud computing, big data, Internet of Things, blockchain, artificial intelligence (AI), virtual reality (VR) and augmented reality (AR), etc. It empowers the construction of high-quality vocational college English courses through enriching the scenario-based applications such as intelligent classroom, adaptive learning, smart diagnosis of students' learning progress, smart classroom evaluations etc., which making the process of higher vocational college English teaching and learning more creative, experiential and inspirational.

However, it is found that at present there are some problems in digitalization empowering the construction of high-quality vocational college English courses, such as teachers' and students' insufficient digital awareness and thinking, insufficient digital infrastructure and equipment in higher vocational colleges and teachers' and students' insufficient digital knowledge and skills.

In order to solve the above-mentioned problems, it is proposed that advanced concepts, reasonable principles and effective methods should be adopted to construct high-quality vocational college English courses empowered by digitalization. The advanced concepts include "fostering virtue and nurturing talents" "student-centered" and "striving for excellence through hard work and comprehensive learning". The reasonable principles involve integration of ideological and political education and the vocational college English teaching, integration of industry and education and school-enterprise cooperation, making English language learning serve the practical purpose and leveraging the role of digital technology in construction of high-quality vocational college English courses. The effective methods include accurately setting teaching objectives, carefully developing teaching materials, carefully organizing teaching implementation, reasonably making teaching assessments and actively building an elite teaching team with the empowerment of digital technologies so as to improve the efficiency and effectiveness of vocational college English teaching, cultivating students' competence to apply English correctly, fluently, and appropriately in cross-cultural communication and achieve good results of English learning.

This book is composed of six chapters. Chapter 1 briefs the background, purpose and significance as well as the organization of the book. Chapter 2 is the literature review and theoretical foundations which mainly explain the connotation of digital empowerment, vocational college English and high-quality courses, as well as the basic theories supporting this study. Chapter 3 gives an analysis of the value, connotation and features of high-quality vocational college

English courses. Chapter 4 gives an exploration on the necessity and feasibility of the construction of high-quality vocational college English courses empowered by digitalization. Chapter 5 gives an analysis of the status quo and countermeasures of the construction of high-quality vocational college English courses empowered by digitalization. Through investigation, it is found that there are some problems in digitalization empowering the construction of high-quality vocational college English courses, such as teachers' and students' insufficient digital awareness and thinking, insufficient digital infrastructure and equipment in higher vocational colleges and insufficient digital literacy and skills of teachers and students. And then it gives an analysis of the causes of the problems in digitalization empowering the construction of high-quality vocational college English courses and puts forward corresponding countermeasures. The final chapter comes to the conclusion. Findings, limitations and suggestions for further study are presented.

It is hoped that this book will provide some useful guidance for the teachers to have a better understanding of the value, connotation and features of high-quality vocational college English courses and learn how to construct high-quality vocational college English courses empowered by digitalization and apply it in their own teaching practice and thus make a valuable contribution towards improving the quality and effects of vocational college English courses.

Due to festinate time, limited knowledge and experience of the author, some mistakes and errors in this book are unavoidable. Feedbacks, comments and suggestions from all readers of this book are warmly welcome so that corrections can be made.

The Author

June 6, 2024

Contents

Chapter 3　Value and Connotation of High-quality Vocational College English Courses ·············053

Chapter 4 Necessity and Feasibility of Construction of High-quality Vocational College English Courses Empowered by Digitalization

Chapter 5 Status Quo and Countermeasures of Construction of High-quality Vocational College English Courses Empowered by Digitalization

Chapter 1

Introduction

1.1　Research Background

1.1.1　Favorable Policy Support for Construction of High-quality Vocational College English Courses

At the beginning of 2019, the State Council of the People's Republic of China issued an implementation plan for the reform of the national vocational education, which stressed that vocational education is equally as important as regular education, and the policies and practices related to vocational education focus more on its distinct characteristics. As a programmatic document for deepening the reform of vocational education in the new era, *Implementation Plan for the Reform of the National Vocational Education* has great influence on China's vocational education. It is conducive to improving recognition for and status of vocational education in the whole society. It can also spur more support and participation in vocational education and guide vocational colleges to deepen reforms and pursue diverse development. A series of decisions and plans have been made by different levels of Chinese government on key issues in the development of vocational education, pointing out the direction for improving the quality of vocation education.

In April 2022, the 34th Session of the Standing Committee of the 13th National People's Congress revised and adopted *Vocational Education Law of the People's Republic of China*, which clearly stated that "Vocational education is a type of education different from and in an important position equal with regular education". It has been legally clarified that vocational education is a type of education. As a type of education, vocational education is different from regular education in terms of teaching, education materials and teachers, etc., and has its own uniqueness.By stressing that vocational education enjoys equal importance to regular education and taking aim at improving the status and attractiveness of vocational education, it calls on governments at different levels to increase funding of vocational education and strengthen the management of teachers and students to create a better learning environment

Courses are the core elements of the high-quality development of vocational education. High-quality courses are the basic units for vocational colleges to cultivate talents and directly affect the quality of cultivation of talents. High-quality courses refer to courses with excellent educational resources, teachers and teaching methods. Since the Ministry of Education first proposed this concept in 2018, how to build high-quality courses has become the focus of all types of education. In the current context of economic globalization and technological progress, the importance of vocational education is becoming increasingly prominent, and it has become imperative to adopt a series of effective measures to build a batch of high-quality courses for vocational education.

1.1.2   Strong Technological Support for Construction of High-quality Vocational College English Courses

The rapid development of digital technologies such as 5G, big data, artificial intelligence, cloud computing and blockchain technology etc., has enabled China's vocational education to accelerate its digital transformation, improving its quality and cultivating highly skilled talent to meet the need of the market. In an era of digital transformation and innovation, with the world being increasingly interconnected by digital technologies, the approaches and effects of vocational college English teaching are undergoing unprecedented changes. The application of digital technologies in vocational college English teaching has improved the quality of English lessons by providing more interesting content and immersive experiences. With the help of digital technologies, the vocational college English teachers can introduce digital teaching methods and resources to enrich the content of English learning and mobilize students' interest in English learning. In addition, it can improve the efficiency and enhance the effectiveness of higher vocational college students' English learning. Digital technology transforming the teaching and learning experience, featured by massive resources and intelligent analysis, will completely change the mode of English teaching and learning. The application of digital technologies will be of great significance for enriching learning resources, improving interaction between teachers and students, and enhancing the scientificity and effectiveness of English learning.

Relying on digital technologies, digital education platform supports students to carry out online learning through computer terminals and mobile terminals. At the same time, it can comprehensively use pictures, audios, videos, interactive activities and other resources to enrich the classroom, stimulate students' learning interest, and increase students' classroom participation degree, and realize the deep reform of English learning in higher vocational colleges. The combination of online and traditional teaching through the application of digital education platform allows students to achieve effective teacher-student interaction and student-student interaction before, during and after class. The application of digital technology can increase the controllability of the teaching process of vocational college English. With the help of digital technology, with unique advantages in individualized learning, differentiated teaching and informed evaluation, higher vocational college English teachers can record the track of students' English learning progress and provide customized teaching schemes for students through information tracking and mining, retrospective digital analysis, scientific monitoring and evaluation. This makes it possible for English teachers in higher vocational colleges to shift their focus from one-way teaching to guiding students' autonomous learning and experiential learning, allowing students to become participants in, rather than spectators of, teaching activities, thus boost students' interests in English learning and improve their English-language proficiency and cross-cultural communication skills.

1.1.3　Sustainable Inherent Need for Improving Quality of Vocational College English Courses

In March 2021, the Ministry of Education of the People's Republic of China released the *English Curriculum Standards for Higher Vocational Education (2021 Edition)* (hereinafter referred to as the "New Curriculum Standards"), stating that the English course for higher vocational education is an integral part of the curriculum system for higher vocational education and is a required or restricted elective course for higher vocational college students with non-English majors. It has both instrumental and humanistic features. It is clarified that the core competencies of the English subject in higher vocational education mainly include four aspects: international communication in the workplace, multi-cultural communication, improvement of linguistic thinking ability, and development of autonomous learning capabilities. Vocational college English teaching plays an important role in fostering students' practical English-language competence, cultural awareness and intercultural communication skills, advancing their cognitive development of language learning so as to better cultivate students' thinking abilities. It is conducive to forging students' global mindset, broadening their international horizons, enhancing their pride and confidence in Chinese culture, and developing the correct outlook on the world, on life and on values.

In today's globalized world, English has become the language of international communication, and has played an increasingly important role in driving China's economic growth and social development. In this context, higher vocational college graduates with good English proficiency will be given greater opportunities for school enrollment, employment and career development. Vocational college English courses are designed to cultivate students' ability to learn and apply English, laying a good English foundation for students' future employment and further study.

In the current era, the scientific and technological revolution and industrial revolution with digital technology as the core driving force are profoundly affecting the process of transformation and upgrading of all walks of life, spawning a series of new needs, new scenarios and new models. They exert great influence in the type of vocational education. Under the background of digital transformation of vocational education, it is imperative that teachers be encouraged to play a leading role in the digital transformation of vocational education and enabled to use digital technologies to improve the efficiency of their teaching. It points out new directions for the improvement of quality of vocational college English, which can be achieved through creating high-quality digital teaching materials, developing high-quality educational resources, building digital teaching platforms, modernizing traditional classroom teaching and learning, designing digital evaluation systems, and establishing digital training systems, etc.

However, the investigation into vocational college English courses found some shortcomings and deficiencies in current teaching reform of higher vocational English courses in some higher vocational colleges such as insufficient teaching resources, insufficient teaching capabilities of teachers, insufficient supply of high-quality teaching content, low flexibility in teaching methods, and incomplete evaluation system, etc., which leads to unsatisfactory effects of vocational college English learning. Digitalization empowerment provides new opportunities for the reform of public English teaching in higher vocational colleges. It plays a very important role in enriching teaching resources, improving teaching capabilities of teachers, enriching teaching content, innovating teaching methods, and improving evaluation systems, and thus help improving the efficiency and enhancing the effectiveness of vocational college English teaching, cultivating students' competence to apply English correctly, fluently, and appropriately in cross-cultural communication and achieve good results of English learning.

1.2   Research Purpose and Significance

1.2.1   Research Purpose

Courses are the core elements of the high-quality development of vocational education. High-quality courses are the basic units for vocational colleges to cultivate talents and directly affect the quality of cultivation of talents. Vocational college English is an integral part of the curriculum system for higher vocational education and is a required or restricted elective course for students in various non-English majors in higher vocational colleges. It has both instrumental and humanistic features. This study intends to explore and practice on building high-quality vocational college English courses empowered by digitalization from aspects such as its value and significance, connotations and characteristics, practical dilemmas and construction paths, etc., aiming to build a high-level, innovative and challenging online and offline integrated course of public English in higher vocational colleges, realizing the organic integration of online teaching and learning with traditional classroom teaching and learning, enabling public English learning in higher vocational colleges to be more attractive and dynamic, allowing students to learn English actively, happily and efficiently, and improving their English language skills.

1.2.2   Research Significance

1. Theoretical significance

Through literature analysis, it was found that although there are many studies on digital empowerment and vocational college English courses, there are very few studies on the integration of digital empowerment and vocational college English courses. No scholars have systematically carried out research and practice on the construction of high-quality vocational college English courses empowered by digitalization. With an exploration on the value and significance, connotation and characteristics, practical challenges and implementation paths of the construction of high-quality vocational college English courses empowered by digitalization, this study has a unique research perspective and broadens the horizon to study English-language teaching and learning.

2. Practical significance

The major practical significance is to deepen the reform of teachers, teaching materials and teaching methods of vocational college English courses. Through a deep exploration on the value and significance, connotation and characteristics, practical challenges and implementation paths of the construction of high-quality vocational college English courses empowered by digitalization, we will lay a good foundation and set a good example for building high-level vocational college English courses. It is beneficial for vocational college English teachers to fully understand, embrace and overcome the challenges brought by digitalization empowering higher vocational public English teaching and learning, and bring into full play digitalization's role in empowering the construction of high-quality vocational college English courses, so as to deepen its reform of teachers, teaching materials and teaching methods.

The second most important practical significance goes to providing students with enjoyable learning experiences and satisfying learning outcomes of vocational college English courses. Digital technology itself does not facilitate learning, but promotes effective learning by supporting learning activities. Any learning occurs in a certain learning situation, but no matter what kind of learning situation, effective learning activities require learners to use digital teaching resources to complete tasks and achieve learning goals within the expected time with the help of teachers and students. Construction of high-quality vocational colleges English courses empowered by digitalization follows the laws of education, teaching process and students' growth, promotes effective learning, and provides students with enjoyable learning experiences and brings satisfying outcomes of vocational college English courses.

Another important practical significance is to improve the effects of public English teaching in vocational colleges. Digital technology, characterized by interconnectivity, high efficiency and real-time dynamic sharing, enriches the scenario-based applications such as intelligent classroom, adaptive learning, smart diagnosis of learning progress, smart classroom evaluations, etc. It can also promote the integration and interaction between traditional classroom education and online education, improving teaching methods and making the English-language teaching and learning process more creative, experiential and inspirational. With the assistance of emerging digital technologies, such as AI, cloud computing, 5G, big data and the internet of things, the learning efficiency of students of vocational college English courses will be improved significantly. In addition, the application of intelligent teaching platforms will be of great significance for enriching teaching resources, improving teaching interaction, and enhancing the scientificity, efficiency and effectiveness of English language teaching.

1.3　Research Organization

This book is composed of six chapters:

Chapter 1 gives an introduction of the background, purpose and significance as well as structure of the book.

Chapter 2 is literature review and theoretical foundations, which mainly explain the connotation of digital empowerment, vocational college English and high-quality courses, as well as the basic theories supporting this study.

Chapter 3 gives an analysis of the value, connotation and features of high-quality vocational college English courses.

Chapter 4 gives an exploration on the necessity and feasibility of the construction of high-quality vocational college English courses empowered by digitalization.

Chapter 5 gives an analysis of the status quo and countermeasures of construction of high-quality vocational college English courses empowered by digitalization. Through investigation, it is found that there are some problems in digitalization empowering the construction of high-quality vocational college English courses, such as teachers and students' insufficient digital awareness and thinking, insufficient digital infrastructure and equipment in higher vocational colleges and insufficient digital literacy and skills of teachers and students. And then it gives an analysis of the causes of the problems in digitalization empowering the construction of high-quality vocational college English courses and puts forward corresponding countermeasures.

The final chapter comes to the conclusion. Findings, limitations of this book as well as suggestions for further study are presented.

Chapter 2

Literature Review and Theoretical Foundations

2.1 Definition of Concepts

2.1.1 Digital Empowerment

Digital empowerment refers to equipping organizations and individuals with the knowledge and skills to navigate our increasingly digitized world. It's about ensuring that everyone and every organization, regardless of their social or economic circumstances, has access to technology and can harness its power for their development. Digital empowerment offers organizations and individuals more capabilities and opportunities with digital technology and digital means to achieve more efficient, innovative and intelligent working practices and lifestyles. Digital empowerment can help organizations and individuals improve efficiency, reduce costs, expand markets, optimize services, and improve user experience.

Its functions are mainly manifested as follows.

（1）To provide affordable and reliable internet connectivity: to ensure that people have access to affordable and reliable internet connectivity, so they can take advantage of the many benefits of the internet, such as access to information, communication, and economic opportunities.

（2）To promote digital literacy and skills development:to provide people with training and resources to develop their digital literacy and skills, they can better utilize digital technologies and the internet to improve their lives and communities.

（3）To create supportive policy environments:to develop policies and initiatives that support the use of digital technologies and the internet, governments and other organizations can promote digital empowerment and encourage the adoption and use of these technologies.

（4）To promote the inclusion and participation of marginalized groups: to work to ensure that marginalized groups, such as women and girls, people with disabilities, and rural communities, have equal access to digital technologies and the internet, they can be more fully included and empowered in the digital economy.

Digital empowerment includes but is not limited to the following aspects.

（1）Data-driven: determined or dependent on the collection or analysis of data, collecting, processing and analyzing data through digital technology to achieve accurate, real-time and effective support for business and decision-making, thereby improving efficiency and competitiveness.

（2）Intelligent application: Through artificial intelligence, machine learning and other technologies, we can realize business process automation, intelligence and intelligent decision-making, and improve production efficiency and service quality.

（3）Internet thinking: The digital economy represented by the Internet emphasizes user-centeredness, with openness, sharing, and collaboration as its basic characteristics, encourages innovation, rapid iteration, and continuous learning, and promotes the rapid development of the digital economy.

（4）Innovative cooperation: Digital empowerment also brings opportunities for innovative cooperation. Through cooperation with other enterprises, organizations and individuals, goals such as resource sharing, business collaboration, and value innovation can be achieved.

The core of digital empowerment is to apply digital technology and digital means to the production, service and management processes of organizations and individuals to achieve more efficient, innovative and intelligent work and lifestyle, thereby improving competitiveness and creating greater success.

2.1.2   Vocational College English Courses

Vocational college English courses, as compulsory courses or restricted elective courses for higher vocational college students of non-English majors, are designed and offered with the aim of cultivating technical and skilled personnel to meet the demands of production, construction, service and management. The objectives of the vocational college English courses are to cultivate students' practical English language proficiency, with a focus on enhancing their cross-cultural communication abilities in workplace scenarios and facilitating the gradual improvement of their English communication competence. Simultaneously, the vocational college English courses will empower students to master effective learning methods and strategies, stimulate their interest in learning and enhance their autonomous learning ability, improve students' comprehensive cultural literacy and awareness of cross-cultural communication, and enhance the students' employment competitiveness for their future sustainable development.

Vocational college English courses not only help students improve their English-language abilities in listening, speaking, reading and writing, but also form a learning system that enables students to achieve a high level of English proficiency. They help foster students' practical language capacity, cultural awareness and intercultural communication skills and also attach great importance to the cognitive development of students' language learning so as to better cultivate their thinking abilities. Vocational colleges set up English courses targeted at training students language communicative competence at workplace settings, take the job requirements as the main thread to develop and construct the teaching content system, adopt teaching modes that reflect the teaching philosophy of "student-centered" and the integration of "teaching, learning and doing", pay attention to developing students' practical language competence, especially the oral communication ability in daily life and future work. Additionally, they should actively introduce and utilize modern teaching facilities such as computers, network technologies, build new teaching modes that are suitable for personalized learning and independent learning, create scene simulations of professional work with the aid of virtual reality technology to enhance the students' workplace communication skills; the schools should adopt flexible and diverse teaching methods, strengthen interactive and collaborative learning to create a favorable learning atmosphere and organize rich and colorful English extracurricular activities, making them an integral part of English teaching.

2.1.3　High-quality Vocational College English Courses

At the National Conference on Undergraduate Education in New Era in 2018, the Minister of Education Chen Baosheng proposed the concept of eliminating "easy courses" and building "high-quality courses". Subsequently, at the Annual International Forum on Higher Education in 2020, the Director of the Department of Higher Education of the Ministry of Education stated that it is necessary to eliminate "easy courses" and create innovative and challenging high-quality courses. The courses are the core elements of talent cultivation, because the quality of the courses directly determines the quality of talent cultivation. The most direct, core and effective way for students to benefit from the universities and colleges is the courses. "Easy courses" are low-level courses that teachers do not pay attention to developing students' interest, or improving their ability to use the knowledge and skills learned. High-quality vocational college English courses are high-level, innovative and challenging English courses. "High-level" refers to the organic integration of knowledge, ability and quality, cultivating students' comprehensive ability and advanced thinking to independently solve complex problems, and shifting from simple transfer of knowledge into a combination of transfer of knowledge, development of skills, and the shaping of character. "Innovative" means that the course content is required to be contemporary and cutting-edge, and can promptly reflect new changes in the industry and future development trends; the teaching modes are both advanced and interactive, and new ideas, new methods, and new means are used to carry out interactive teaching. The learning results are exploratory and personalized, achieving the results of the unity of knowledge and action, the unity of learning and thinking, and the development of personality. "Challenging" means that academic workload and difficulty with certain degree must be increased in higher vocational college English courses to add more pressure for higher vocational college students, so that the students not only need to pay close attention during class, but also conduct extra learning after school.

2.1.4 Construction of High-quality Vocational College English Courses Empowered by Digitalization

Construction of high-quality vocational college English courses empowered by digitalization mainly involves three aspects: technological empowerment, platform empowerment and psychological empowerment. The starting point of technological empowerment and platform empowerment is to maximize the advantages and benefits of technology and platforms to help vocational college English teachers and students stimulate psychological empowerment, bring their initiatives into full play and improve the quality of English teaching and learning through reforming traditional classroom teaching and learning and making more high-quality digital textbooks and teaching materials accessible to learners with the help of digital technologies such as 5G, big data, artificial intelligence, cloud computing and blockchain technology etc.

1. Technological empowerment

Technological empowerment means that digital technologies such as 5G, big data, artificial intelligence, cloud computing and blockchain technology provide digital technology support during the teaching process of higher vocational college English, thereby showing certain advantages. The advantages can be manifested from the perspectives of teachers and students. From the perspective of higher vocational college English teachers, technological empowerment is helpful for them to change their teaching concepts. Educational modernization calls for the integration of information technology into curriculum teaching. Governments, schools, and teachers have shown great enthusiasm and interest in the integration of information technology and curriculum teaching, providing a good opportunity for teachers to change their teaching concepts. Technological empowerment can help achieve diversification of public English teaching methods in higher vocational colleges. Currently, the most widely used teaching method is multimedia teaching. With the continuous development and innovation of digital technology, various teaching methods such as electronic distance teaching, online classroom, flipped classroom, and blended teaching are increasingly widely used by teachers in public English teaching in higher vocational colleges. It can make the connection between teaching and guidance, learning and practice smoother, and the effect of vocational college English teaching more obvious. From the perspective of higher vocational college students, technological empowerment offers an engaging and convenient way to expand their knowledge, develop their language skills, fostering personal growth and professional development, and allows them to access a wide range of teaching resources at their fingertips, giving them the freedom to learn at their own pace and on their own terms. It brings the following benefits to them.

（1）Flexibility: Learn on their own schedule and keep a balance between work, study, and other commitments.

（2）Accessibility: Access teaching materials anytime, anywhere – all they need are internet connections.

（3）Personalized learning: Tailor their vocational college English learning to meet specific needs or goals through customized lessons or tutoring sessions.

（4）Cost-effective: Save money by eliminating the need for travel or purchase of expensive textbooks while often gaining access to free or lower-cost resources.

（5）Collaboration opportunities: Interact with instructors, tutors, English teachers and fellow students from around the world in real-time discussions or forums.

2. Platform empowerment

A digital platform is an internet-based technology that allows businesses or individuals to connect and exchange data, knowledge and experiences (Hsieh & Wu, 2019). Kozinets et al. (2021) summarize the empowering role of online platforms as pertaining to strengthening or enabling abilities and providing collective spaces. Ye and Yang (2020) highlight two potential outcomes of platform empowerment: the bridging of digital divides and the promise of greater social inclusion. Platform empowerment refers to providing resources and functional support for the public English teaching in higher vocational colleges through teaching platforms, mainly focusing on the resources, functions, etc. There are many types of teaching platforms, which are mainly divided into two categories. One is online platforms, such as MOOC platform, NetEase Vopen platform, etc.; the other is online-to-offline platforms, such as Superstar Learning platform, Rain Classroom platform, and Mosoteach platform, etc. These platforms rely on various information technologies and integrate them into the platform, making the functions of the platform more novel and powerful, thus highlighting the advantages of the platform in empowering the teaching of public English courses in higher vocational colleges. Platform empowerment helps integrate and share resources in higher vocational college English courses. For example, the Superstar Learning platform integrates multiple resources and provides a wealth of digital resources. Teachers of higher vocational college English can search for the materials they need to assist in lesson preparation and teaching. Higher vocational college students can also access to resources which are interesting to them from the platform, which not only broadens the ways to acquire knowledge, but also widens the scope of knowledge and skills. Platform empowerment helps to diversify the interaction between teachers and students and among students in higher vocational college English teaching and learning. For example, the Superstar Learning platform and the Mosoteach platform have various interactive methods such as random selection, answering questions, questionnaires, voting, discussions, and live broadcasts. Additionally, these platforms combine PowerPoint and WeChat for sharing teaching materials and communication. Students can receive video, audio and school work files on WeChat and ask questions live during the class. It is conducive to increasing students' participation and enthusiasm, and is also conducive to improving the efficiency of higher vocational college English teaching. Platform empowerment helps to broaden the channels for teachers and students of higher vocational college English to obtain resources, diversify teaching and learning interactions, and also helps to provide teaching and learning support.

3. Psychological empowerment

Psychological empowerment is a motivational state involving four dimensions: meaning, competence, self-determination and impact (Spreitzer, 1995). Meaning indicates the degree to which individuals perceive their work is significant or meaningful. Competence refers to one's ability, skills and capabilities to accomplish their work. Self-determination is one's perception of having choice at work and freedom on how they do their job. Impact concerns the perceived influence of one's work on the organization or department. Technology empowerment and platform empowerment emphasize the use of external means to assist higher vocational college English teachers and students, while psychological empowerment focuses on the inner psychological state of the teachers and students. The essence of the psychological empowerment process can be described as being based on motivation, allowing the subject to feel the changes brought about by empowerment, have a sense of subjective empowerment, enhance social psychology and intrinsic motivation, and improve the subject's personal beliefs and self-efficacy. The concept of self-efficacy was proposed by psychologist Albert Bandura, who believed that self-efficacy is a reflection of one's own self-confidence. Self-efficacy has different effects in different domains. In higher vocational colleges, the self-efficacy of teachers and students will affect teaching and learning effects. Higher vocational college English teachers can take advantages of digital technology and platform empowerment to enhance their self-efficacy in the teaching process, improve digital technology literacy, and improve their level of education and teaching, and consequently improve the quality of English teaching in higher vocational colleges. For some higher vocational students who deem that they entered higher vocational colleges due to poor academic performance, resulting in low self-esteem and a lack of confidence in learning higher vocational college English, technological empowerment and platform empowerment are effective in helping them obtain abundant high-quality teaching resources, advance the reform of learning methods, developing their practical language competence, especially the oral communication ability in daily life and future work, thus increasing their self-confidence, enhancing self-efficacy and positive attitudes in learning higher vocational college English. Through psychological empowerment, the self-efficacy of higher vocational college English teachers and students can be effectively improved, thereby continuously improving the quality, efficiency and effect of public English teaching in higher vocational colleges.

To sum up, technological empowerment is to provide digital technology support for teachers and students in higher vocational college English; platform empowerment is to provide resource and functional support for them on the basis of technological empowerment; psychological empowerment focuses on intrinsic task motivation reflecting a sense of self-control in relation to one's work and an active involvement with one's work role. It improves the psychological state of the empowered teachers and students, enhances their self-efficacy, and gives them a sense of existence, achievement and happiness. Technological empowerment, platform empowerment, and psychological empowerment are closely linked, have intertwined with and influenced each other. Platform empowerment is the carrier of technological empowerment. Technological empowerment needs to use certain platforms to display the empowerment effect, while psychological empowerment needs to be maximized through taking effective measures to utilize and leverage the advantages of technology and platforms to provide psychological support to the empowered teachers and students of higher vocational college English.

2.2　Literature Review

2.2.1　Literature Review on Digital Empowerment

1. Literature review on the concept of digital empowerment

Digital empowerment is developed from the concept of empowerment. Empowerment is a management concept that can result in higher productivity and job satisfaction in the organization. Empowerment is the concept in management that if employees are given information, resources, and opportunity at the same time as being held responsible for their job outcomes, then they will be more productive and have higher job satisfaction. It is important to understand that a company cannot implement empowerment itself; instead, management creates the right environment so that empowerment can take place. Since its first proposal in the 1970s, the concept of empowerment is of increasing interest to researchers, practitioners and citizens. An increased interest in empowerment has been seen in diverse subject areas within psychology and management, including motivation, task performance, leadership, group processes, decision-making, and organizational design, because empowerment can enhance employee performance, well-being, and positive attitudes of individuals, teams, and organizations.

Whitmore (1988) defines empowerment as an interactive process through which people experience personal and social change, enabling them to take action to achieve influence over the organizations and institutions which affect their lives and the communities in which they live.

Keiffer (1984) labels empowerment as a developmental process which includes four stages, namely entry, advancement, incorporation, and commitment. The first stage, entry stage, appears to be motivated by the participant's experience of some event or condition threatening to the self or family, what Keiffer refers to as an act of "provocation". In the following advancement stage, there are three major aspects which are important to continuing the empowerment process: a mentoring relationship; supportive peer relationships with a collective organization; and the development of a more critical understanding of social and political relations. The central focus of the third stage appears to be the development of a growing political consciousness. Commitment is the final stage in which the participants apply the new participatory competence to ever expanding areas of their lives.

According to Wallerstein (1992), empowerment is a social-action process that promotes participation of people, organizations, and communities towards the goals of increased individual and community control, political efficacy, improved quality of community life, and social justice. Whitmore (1988) feels the concept of empowerment needs to be more clearly defined and she defined empowerment as processes whereby individuals achieve increasing control of various aspects of their lives and participate in the community with dignity.

Rappaport's (1987) concept of empowerment conveys both a psychological sense of personal control or influence and a concern with actual social influence, political power and legal rights. In this sense, empowerment can exist at three levels: at the personal level, where empowerment is the experience of gaining increasing control and influence in daily life and community participation (Keiffer, 1984); at the small group level, where empowerment involves the shared experience, analysis, and influence of groups on their own efforts (Presby, Wandersman, Florin, Rich & Chavis, 1990); and at the community level, where empowerment revolves around the utilization of resources and strategies to enhance community control (Labonte, 1989).

Digital empowerment refers to equipping individuals or organizations with the knowledge and skills to navigate our increasingly digitized world. It's about ensuring that everyone or every organization, regardless of their social or economic circumstances, has access to technology and can harness its power for their development. Digital empowerment's essentially about equipping everyone or organization with the necessary digital skills and internet access, enabling them to participate in today's tech-driven world fully. It's a movement that aims to level the playing field by providing equal opportunities for all individuals or organizations, regardless of their socioeconomic status or geographic location. Its primary goal is to bridge the digital divide and provide everyone or organization with the tools they need to succeed in this digital age.

In the context of digital age, the progress of China's digital technology has brought empowerment to various industries and fields, promoted the development of society, organizations, and individuals, and attracted many scholars' attention to the concept of "empowerment". Although scholars have not given a unified definition of digital empowerment, several domestic scholars such as Chen Haibei

(2019), Hu Chunhui (2020), Gao Hui (2020), and Li Zhuojun (2021) believe that digital empowerment refers to giving certain powers or abilities to organizations, institutions or individuals through various digital technologies, methods and tools. Chen Haibei (2019) believes that digital empowerment is not only a behavior or measure, but also a process. Through digital empowerment, people can acquire corresponding life skills and survivability and combat capabilities. Hu Chunhui (2020) and Li Zhuojun (2021) believe that digital empowerment can improve the efficiency of handling things. Gao Huijun (2021) believes that digital empowerment is a concept that comes with Internet technology, but it is also a comprehensive concept. Digital technology is only one dimension, and there should be other dimensions, such as thinking and cognition, organizational management and practical application. To sum up, digital empowerment emphasizes giving subjects more powerful capabilities through the use of digital technology and digital tools.

2. Application research on digital empowerment of development of vocational education

In recent years, many countries and international organizations around the world have rolled out a series of national-level digital development strategies to promote a comprehensive digital transformation in education, promote innovation in digital education and make it more equitable, inclusive and of higher quality. They aim to promote the high-quality development of digital education, promote the all-around development of people and the advancement of society and civilization, and make greater contribution to the building of a community with a shared future for mankind. For example, UK released "Realizing the Potential of Technology in Education: A Strategy for Education Providers and the Technology Industry" (2019); the European Union released "the Digital Education Action Plan (2021-2027) " (2021); the United States released "Advancing Digital Equity for All: Community-based Recommendations for Developing Effective Digital Equity Plans to Close the Digital Divide and Enable Technology-Empowered Learning"

(2022); Germany released "Charter for Digital Education Innovation" (2022); Canada released "Digital Learning Strategy" (2022), France released the "2023-2027 Education Digitalization Strategy" (2023).

Over recent years, the Chinese government also proposed a series of strategies and policies aimed at further promoting the systematic integration of intelligent technology and education. These include China's Education Modernization 2035 Plan, the New Generation Artificial Intelligence Development Plan, and Education Informatization 2.0 Action Plan. In addition, the Ministry of Education of the People's Republic of China also stressed the importance of implementing the strategic action of education digitalization as well as accelerating the process of digital transformation and intelligent upgrade of education.

In the report of the 20th National Congress of the Communist Party of China (CPC), it is emphasized that "promoting the digitalization of education, building a learning society and a learning nation with lifelong learning for all" (2022). Through literature review, it can be found that few foreign scholars have conducted systematic research on digital empowerment of vocational education; while domestic scholars started research on digital empowerment of vocational education relatively late. It was not until 2011 that papers on related themes and topics emerged. Subsequently, some domestic scholars have carried out application research on digital empowerment of vocational education and gain fruitful research results. Li Zhuojun (2021) pointed out that digitalization empowerment facilitates the reform of teaching methods, promotes the construction and sharing of teaching resources, and improves teachers' digital literacy. Li Xiaojuan and Wang Yi (2021) pointed out that technology empowers the cultivation of teachers' digital literacy in vocational colleges, including empowering teachers to cultivate digital craftsmen, empowering teachers to carry out multi-modal teaching, empowering teachers' classroom digital management and evaluation, and empowering teachers' application and development of digital resources. Zhang Qingshan (2022) elaborated on the transformation trend of digital empowerment of vocational education, analyzed the process of digital empowerment, and proposed the positive effects of digital empowerment of high-quality development of vocational education from the aspects of personalization, socialization, ubiquity, and gridding in order to promote the high-quality development of vocational education. He Shuxia, Sun Chao, and Ji Tao (2024) pointed out that digital empowerment of the integration of industry and education in the vocational education sector possesses the characteristics of "dataization", "platformization", "interaction", and "collaboration". They also proposed that the improvement strategies for the digital empowerment of the integration of industry and education in the vocational education sector comprise exploring new concepts for the integration of industry and education, enriching the content of industry-education integration, reconstructing the industry-education integration community through the application of digital and intelligent technologies, and integrating resources to enhance data application capabilities.

Higher vocational college English is an integral part of the curriculum system for higher vocational education and is a required or restricted elective course for students in various non-English majors. It has the characteristics of universality, instrumentality and humanism with the goal of fostering students' practical language capacity in workplace scenarios, especially their listening and speaking ability. At the same time, it aims to improve students' comprehensive cultural literacy and cross-cultural communication awareness, cultivate students' learning interest and independent learning capabilities, enable students to master effective learning methods and strategies, and lay the foundation for improving students' employment competitiveness and future sustainable development.

Some scholars have carried out research on the construction of higher vocational college English courses empowered by digitalization and achieved a series of research results. Dong Yanan (2021) discussed the paths to enhance professional capabilities of English teachers in higher vocational colleges under the background of digitalization, and pointed out that digital transformation is a trend in English teaching in higher vocational colleges and hence we should establish advanced teaching concepts, update talent cultivation plans, optimize curriculum systems, strengthen supervision in teaching, innovate talent cultivation models, teaching models and teaching methods, enhance teachers' professional capabilities, promote digital transformation, boost students' knowledge, and raise students' interest in learning and achieve the goals of English teaching in higher vocational colleges.

Gao Chong and Xiang Chengdong (2023) pointed out that in the era of digital economy, the teaching of English courses in higher vocational colleges needs to be reshaped through digital empowerment. Application of digital resources such as learning by scanning the QR code, taking online courses via online education platform, using mobile applications, applying micro-lesson resources, and data mining empower the reform of English teaching in higher vocational colleges, help improve teaching quality, efficiency and effectiveness, and can make up for the shortcomings of English teaching in higher vocational colleges.

From the above analysis, we can see that scholars both at home and abroad have carried out in-depth research on digital empowerment of vocational education and achieved some research results, laying a solid foundation for the reform and innovation of vocational courses through digital empowerment.

However, currently there are only a handful of papers on the reform of higher vocational college English empowered by digitalization, which also shows that research on the reform of higher vocational college English empowered by digitalization needs to be further deepened and improved, and currently no systematic study have been carried out on construction of high-quality vocational college English courses empowered by digitalization.

2.2.2 Literature Review on Vocational College English Courses

1. Literature review on vocational college English courses in foreign countries

Foreign research on public English started early. D. Hymes and H. Dell (1972) proposed that English professional capability is continuously accumulated and improved in the process of English learning, and is a dynamic development process. Hutchinson T. and Waters A. (1987) mentioned that English learning is a kind of learning for the purpose of communication based on various needs such as employment, work, and career. For the first time, they classify English into three categories according to their specific purposes, namely "English for science and technology", "business English" and "English for social sciences". Harris Alma (2006) once proposed that in English teaching in higher vocational colleges, in addition to imparting knowledge about foreign languages to students, it is also necessary to expand their extracurricular practical knowledge according to their different majors, with emphasis on fostering students' practical language capacity. Elizabeth Platt (1996) studied the cooperation between vocational skills teachers and vocational English training teachers in an environment that simulated working scenarios, and designed teaching plan through learning by doing approach with an expectation to improve learners' English language ability. Carter Amanda G., Creedy Debra K. and Sidebotham Mary (2016) took the nursing major as an example and pointed out that the written English teaching cases can cultivate the competence of nursing students to apply English in real medical scenarios. Teaching design based on real working scenarios should gradually replace that of traditional English language teaching. S. Bosher and K. Smallkosk designed the English practical training course "Listening and Speaking in Healthcare Scenarios" during teaching to allow students to raise their competence to apply English in real medical scenarios.

Australia implements the modern apprenticeship system, which requires students to spend 80% of their study time in working positions and the remaining time in school. The course content is rich and has strong practicality and professionalism. Japan began to attach more importance to English earlier than our country, as early as at the end of the 20th century.

Japanese scholars have a clear idea that the lack of or low proficiency in foreign language will lead to the derailment of national development and the world.

Since then, Japan has vigorously promoted the learning of foreign languages and regarded it as an important measure for the development of national education. Famous Japanese educator Takagi Kuyo found that students in the school's medical department are not satisfied with public English teaching through questionnaire data analysis, mainly because the public English courses and teaching content set by the school for these students have little relevance to the medical majors.

Based on this problem, Takagi Kuyo redesigned and rearranged the public English course teaching from both the course and teaching content, and applied it to classroom practice, and the effect was significantly improved. Occupational English is very popular in countries where English is not the native language, and more and more learners hope to promote their future career development through learning English knowledge related to working positions.

2. Literature review on vocational college English courses in China

Research on vocational college English courses in China mainly focuses on the following aspects:

（1）Research on the dilemma of vocational college English courses in China.

Zhang Yue (2013) discussed the dilemma of vocational college English courses in China. The problems faced by vocational college English courses are insufficient English teaching materials and fixed teaching methods, mainly based on traditional models and lack of modernity; shortage of teaching staff; the weak teaching capacity of English teachers; mismatch between the teaching staff and the actual teaching needs etc. Based on these problems, he proposed a series of countermeasures. For example, we must deepen teaching reforms, including revising textbooks, changing teaching methods, conducting diversified teaching reforms, conducting quality improvement training for English teachers, and improving the quality of English teaching in higher vocational colleges. Ma Qiong and Song Zhengfu (2021) proposed that summative assessments based on final exams are not conducive to higher vocational students rebuilding their confidence in learning. Teachers should change the concept of education, break the "scores-only" evaluation model in traditional teaching, and look for new models in evaluating the performance of students, allowing students to improve their learning abilities and maximize their learning potential, thereby helping them achieve continuous progress and improvement in their English language abilities.

（2）Research on teaching methods and techniques for vocational college English courses.

In recent years, research on English teaching in higher vocational colleges has been focuses on innovation and development of teaching methods and teaching techniques for higher vocational colleges. Many famous teachers in China have gained profound research outcomes in this field. However, judging from the overall learning effect of higher vocational college students, the teaching methods and teaching techniques of English teaching in higher vocational colleges are still far from satisfactory, and there is still big room for improvement. Yan Bingxiang, an authoritative domestic expert, once expressed his disappointment with English teaching in higher vocational colleges in China. He deemed that English teaching in China lacks its own uniqueness and the positioning of English teaching is very vague. Almost English teaching in all higher vocational colleges adopts the same teaching methods and techniques and doesn't have its own characteristics. Educator Shi Rui had also expressed his dissatisfaction with the current English teaching methods. He deemed that most of the English teaching methods used by higher vocational college English teachers are piling up words and translating articles. Students are forced to become "living dictionary" through study, and they are very resistant to English, and they are even more dissatisfied with this learning method. In the classroom, it is very difficult for teachers to inspire students' enthusiasm for learning English, and it gradually becomes a burden for vocational college students to bear.

Another scholar, Dai Zhuo, elaborated on what he believed to be the most efficient way to learn English. In learning, one must first put their learning into practice to achieve the goal of applying what one has learned. At the same time, teachers must gradually learn to attract students' attention in the classroom, creating an atmosphere to inspire students' enthusiasm for learning English, and guide students to participate in classroom activities, so that students can actively participate in all aspects of English language learning such as listening, speaking, reading, writing and translating. Students take the initiative to learn English and can spontaneously participate in some English competitions and activities, thereby foster a strong atmosphere of English learning and improving students' learning abilities and effects.

Zhu Ying and Liu Zhenping (2020) pointed out that strengthening the experience based on working scenarios in English classes is a new requirement for English teaching in the new era. The core of realizing the transformation of English classroom from learners' "observation" to learners' "experience" is to give learning assignments related to language application in working scenarios according to the needs of learners, and then guide learners to build a learning community and transform learning assignments into learning experience with personalized meanings, which can meet learners' real needs and promote learners' development in their English language abilities.

（3）Research on the training of vocational college English teachers.

English teachers are the carriers of imparting English knowledge. The training of vocational college English teachers is a necessary and effective way to improve the efficiency of English teaching. Liu Yue (2019) pointed out that English teachers in higher vocational colleges are called high-quality English language educators. They must match their English competence and knowledge to students' needs, and more importantly, they must master systematic teaching theories and methods. In addition, English teachers in higher vocational colleges must also master competence and knowledge related to their majors. However, the current problem in teaching faculty faced by higher vocational colleges is mainly the lack of front-line teachers with work experience and teaching characteristics and styles. The main reason for this situation is that teacher recruitment only focuses on academic qualifications and lack of practice. Most English teachers only master the necessary knowledge and skills to teach English rather than those related to students' specific majors.

Teng Chunyan (2020) discussed the opportunities, problems and solutions for the internationalization development of vocational college English teachers under the background of the Belt and Road Initiative, and pointed out that under this background, the application scenarios of English have expanded and the demand for English professionals has increased, and the channels for improving the competence and quality of vocational college English teachers are constantly enriched, providing opportunities for the internationalization development of vocational college English teachers. However, currently there are some practical problems in the internationalization of teaching faculty of vocational college English courses such as lack of scientific planning, imperfect training mechanism, unreasonable teaching faculty, and backward teacher evaluation system. It is proposed to strengthen top-level design, improve training mechanisms, innovate personnel systems, and improve evaluation system, in order to help vocational college English teachers achieve internationalization development.

（4）Research on teaching models of vocational college English courses.

In China, the typical research on teaching models of higher vocational college English is Mei Hongju's "A Brief Analysis of the Hierarchical Teaching of Vocational College English", in which she proposed that traditional vocational college English teaching model should be transformed and hierarchical teaching models are adopted in the classroom according to the students' different aptitudes. Wang Liusha (2016) proposed using multimedia network technology to create a learning atmosphere in English classes and change the way of learning English. It can also improve the quality of teaching and lay a foundation for students to achieve lifelong learning even after graduating from colleges.

Yi Hongbo (2023) pointed out that China is making progress in expanding enrollment in vocational colleges. Previously consisting primarily of high school and secondary vocational school graduates, students who pursue higher vocational education now boast diverse backgrounds, including demobilized military personnel, laid-off workers and migrant workers etc. The diversified backgrounds of higher vocational college students will inevitably lead to students' uneven English proficiency, and their different English learning needs. However, due to limitations of teaching management and teachers' qualifications, there are still some problems in higher vocational college English teaching such as the traditional classroom teaching in which a single teacher faces a class of at least 30 students, making it impossible for teachers to give feedback and professional advice to every student. It is proposed that based on students' needs and employers' requirements, new teaching models be constructed to further deepen the reform of English teaching in higher vocational colleges by providing students with an enjoyable learning experience and a satisfying learning outcome, so as to cultivate versatile talents with solid professional knowledge and strong English language abilities.

（5）Research on the influence of higher vocational college English skills competitions on promoting the reform of English teaching.

In higher vocational colleges in China, English teaching and research groups often hold various English skills competitions, mainly aiming to enhance students' enthusiasm for learning English and concurrently facilitate teachers' advancements in English teaching. Chen Xiangyun (2017) conducted a detailed analysis of the English skills competition in "Exploration of College English Classroom Teaching under the Core Competency System". Through research, he concluded that the development of English skills competitions gradually adapts to the reform of English teaching. He believes that the English skills competition in higher vocational colleges in China can reversely promote the reform of English teaching in higher vocational colleges and make English teaching more practical and life-oriented. The main purpose of holding various English vocational skills competitions is to use the competitions to improve students' practical English abilities. In English skills competitions and English teaching, schools and teachers must integrate the English teaching models, teaching objectives and student evaluation systems with the needs of social development. By combining it with practice students can master it, and the ultimate goal is to enable students to quickly adapt to the English application environment when they are employed in the future.

Based on the comparison of studies on public English teaching in higher vocational colleges at home and abroad, it can be found that academic research on English teaching in higher vocational colleges is from multiple perspectives and at various levels, including the characteristics, connotation and content of English teaching in higher vocational colleges. Literature review on higher vocational college English teaching both at home and abroad can provide relevant theoretical basis and reference for this study. At the same time, it was also discovered that there are still some gaps in the academic research results on English teaching in higher vocational colleges. In particular, no scholars have yet conducted systematic research on the construction of high-quality vocational college English courses empowered by digitalization.

2.2.3   Literature Review on Construction of High-quality Courses

At the National Conference on Undergraduate Education in New Era in 2018, the Minister of Education Chen Baosheng proposed the concept of eliminating "easy courses" and building "high-quality courses". Subsequently, at the Annual International Forum on Higher Education in 2020, the Director of the Department of Higher Education of the Ministry of Education stated that it is necessary to eliminate "easy courses" and create innovative and challenging "high-quality courses". "High-quality courses" has quickly become a hot word and hot topic in the field of education. Extensive and in-depth discussions have been conducted on them in the academic circle, mainly focusing on the following four aspects.

1. Research on the connotation of "high-quality courses"

Different scholars have different ideas regarding the definition of "high-quality course", mainly from the following three aspects: Firstly, understand the "high-quality course" from its constituent elements. Wu Yan holds that "high-quality courses" are first-class demonstration courses. Li Zhiyi (2018) believes that a classroom featuring "exploration, criticality, dialogue, openness, and the integration of knowledge and practice" can be proposed as the constituent elements of the "high-quality course". Secondly, understand the "high-quality course" through the management of the school. Colleges and universities should emphasize their characteristics when designing and implementing curricula. Thirdly, comprehend the "high-quality course" through its connotation. "High-level" indicates the high quality and profound connotation of the "high-quality course", "innovative" highlights the uniqueness and cutting-edge nature of the "high-quality course", and "challenging" reflects the exploratory connotation of the "high-quality course". Deng Zhongbo (2020) deems that "high-quality courses" have well-organized teaching content and are student-centered and outcome-based.

2. Research on the constitutive elements of "high-quality courses"

The constitutive elements are the most common influencing factors in the construction of the "high-quality courses". Many scholars believe that the construction of "high-quality courses" is a systematic task involving teachers, teaching content and teaching methods etc., and institutional incentives need to be integrated throughout the entire teaching process. Yu Tingzhong (2020) believes that the key to the construction of "high-quality courses" is to form a top-notch teaching team. Teachers' classroom teaching is the most authoritative and convenient way for students to acquire knowledge. The status of teachers' classroom teaching determines the effectiveness of teaching. Liu Wenkai (2020) believes that the "high-quality courses" should not merely teach basic theories and knowledge but also impart abundant and cutting-edge knowledge, cultivate students' innovative thinking and enhance their innovative spirit and practical abilities. The course content must integrate professional education with ideological and political education, ensuring that the talents cultivated possess not only professional qualities but also firm ideals and beliefs. The course content must be contemporary and cutting-edge, concentrating on how theoretical knowledge can exert an effect on new industry developments via modern science and technology, and meet the demands of diversified talents. Zhu Shanyuan (2023) puts forward that the components of the high-quality courses in higher vocational colleges encompass five elements: teachers, teaching materials, teaching and learning conditions, students, and learning evaluations. Teachers are the implementers and leaders in the construction of high-quality courses; moreover, favorable teaching and learning conditions are the guarantee for the construction of high-quality courses; students are the participants in the construction of high-quality courses.

3. Research on the difficulties faced during the construction of "high-quality courses"

Hu Wanshan (2019) holds the opinion that teachers in Chinese colleges and universities have not fully employed the "high-quality courses" construction policies. The current difficulties they encounter during course construction include the weak awareness of the course construction team, the insufficiency of high-quality course resources, the inadequate awareness and insufficient supportive measures of online course construction. Xie Youru (2019) deems that the current design of course content reflects the systematic nature of knowledge, yet it lacks cutting-edge scientific research and applied knowledge. The inclusiveness of the content is weak and fails to meet the needs of applied and academic talents. Bo Rongrong (2019) holds the view that in light of the current situation of tightened entry restrictions and relaxed exit restrictions in undergraduate education, the teaching objectives are not accurately grasped, and teachers fail to master the teaching methods. The teacher-centered lecture, the most common teaching method, makes students only passive learners. The long-term insufficient subjective consciousness of students and the gradually weakening awareness of their participation in after-school learning activities are obstacles to the implementation of the "high-quality courses" at present. Lan Shui (2023) believes that since the construction of high-quality ideological and political courses in higher vocational colleges is still in the preliminary exploration stage and in practice confronts the dilemma of lacking "clear awareness" at the conceptual level, lacking "solid guarantee" at the basic level, and lacking "information-driven" at the methodological aspect. Therefore, it is necessary to establish the concept of ideological and political education and construct a distinctive "high-quality course", lay a solid foundation for ideological and political courses and construct a standard "high-quality courses", and enrich ideological and political education methods and construct an intelligent "high-quality courses" .

4. Research on the paths of constructing "high-quality courses"

Deng Li (2018) holds the opinion that inquiry is the key to driving complex thinking and advanced thinking. Training advanced thinking is the outcome of the construction of "high-quality courses", and the construction results should be reflected in students' achievements. Xue Ruili (2019) deems that only by promoting the transformation of teaching concepts and models and normalizing flipped classroom teaching, and introducing a teaching assistant system in classroom teaching, which is good at discovering problems and assisting teachers in handling daily affairs, can teachers concentrate most of their efforts on teaching arrangements to improve the quality of teaching reform. Zhu Shanyuan (2023) proposes to implement the top-level teaching design empowered by digitalization from a high starting point, optimize the intelligent teaching environment with high standards, build a structured teaching innovation team at a high level, develop digital teaching resources of high quality, create personalized high-quality online courses, and conduct high-precision diagnosis and monitoring of teaching quality. Implement the construction of "high-quality courses" with digital teaching to make it more interactive and attractive to students, and achieve the reform goals of enhancing teachers' sense of accomplishment in teaching and students' sense of gain in learning, as well as improving the quality of school operation and talent cultivation.

To sum up, although the research results on digital empowerment, vocational college English, and high-quality courses both domestically and internationally are considerable, there are few studies on the construction of vocational college English empowered by digitalization. No systematic research on the construction of high-quality vocational college English courses has been conducted yet. However, the investigation into vocational college English courses revealed some shortcomings and deficiencies in the current teaching reform of public English courses in some higher vocational colleges, such as insufficient learning resources, inadequate teaching capabilities of teachers, insufficient supply of high-quality teaching content, low flexibility in teaching methods, and incomplete evaluation system, etc., which leads to unsatisfactory effects of vocational college English learning. Conducting research and practice on the construction of high-quality vocational college English courses empowered by digitalization will help teachers of higher vocational college English to fully utilize digital empowerment to build rich, diverse, and vivid course resources, enhance its ideological and political education, optimize the supply of course content, innovate teaching methods, and improve the evaluation system. Thus, the high-quality vocational college English course with an extensive range of teaching resources, profound teaching content, lively classroom atmosphere, effective teaching and learning results, will enable the students to learn actively, joyfully, and efficiently, and thereby enhance the teaching quality of higher vocational college English courses.

2.3 Theoretical Foundations

2.3.1 Constructivist Learning Theory

Constructivism is a theory of knowledge (epistemology) that argues that humans generate knowledge and meaning from an interaction between their experiences and their ideas. During infancy, it is an interaction between their experiences and their reflexes or behavior-patterns. Piaget called these systems of knowledge schemata. Saul McLeod (2024) holds the opinion that constructivism is a learning theory that puts emphasis on the active role of learners in building their own understanding. Rather than passively receiving information, learners engage in reflection upon their own experiences, create mental representations, and incorporate new knowledge into their schemas, which facilitates deeper learning and understanding. Piaget's theory of constructivist learning has exerted wide-ranging impacts on learning theories and teaching methods in education and is an underlying theme of many education reform movements. Elliott (2000) states that constructivism is "an approach to learning that people actively construct or make their own knowledge and that reality is determined by the experiences of the learner". In elaborating on constructivists' ideas, Arends (1998) states that constructivism holds that the learner personally constructs meaning through experience, and that meaning is influenced by the interaction between prior knowledge and new events.

Constructivist learning theory underpins a variety of student-centered teaching methods and techniques which contrast with traditional education, whereby knowledge is simply passively transmitted by teachers to students. When implementing the constructivist theory in the classroom, lessons must include the following components:

（1）Eliciting prior knowledge. Since new understanding is constructed upon pre-existing knowledge, teachers must initially activate students' prior knowledge, which can be achieved through collaborative activities, relaxed discussions, or pre-tests.

（2）Creating cognitive dissonance. Knowledge is built when new ideas are presented and activities are just challenging enough for students. "Just right problems" force students to reevaluate the schemas in their mind and organize new solutions.

（3）Applying knowledge with feedback. The role of teachers is to encourage students and provide feedback, which can be seen in the form of quizzes, presentations, or discussions in the classroom. The objective of applying feedback should be to stimulate even more growth and challenge knowledge of the new situation.

（4）Reflecting on learning. Students should be provided with the opportunities to reflect on their understanding and showcase their learning, which may be in the form of essays, presentations, or even the responsibilities of sharing their knowledge with other students.

What's more, there are four key areas that are vital for the success of a constructivist classroom: the teacher assumes the role of a facilitator rather than a director; there are equal authority and responsibility between the students and the teacher; learning takes place in small groups; knowledge is shared between both the students and the teacher. These four areas must be tackled in order for the constructivist classroom to be successful. It can be seen clearly that a constructivist classroom differs greatly from the traditional classroom. Constructivist classrooms are more student-centered and the learning revolves around their interests and questions. Teachers guide learning by carrying out group activities, creating collaborative dialogues, and facilitating interactive experiences. Students build upon their prior knowledge and construct new understanding based on the lessons imparted. Dialogues and negotiations are also crucial elements for successful learning.

The major implications of applying the constructivist learning theory in the construction of high-quality vocational college English courses are listed below. As facilitators, the higher vocational college English teachers must bring into full play the digital technology, promote collaborations and adjust their lessons based on their prior understanding of the class, and create a welcoming environment that promotes students' active engagement in learning. Specifically, higher vocational college English teachers need to give full play to the role of digital technology, establish scientific and efficient learning scenarios for college students, and increase their awareness and ability to actively build knowledge and construct new understanding upon their prior knowledge and experience; on the other hand, effective measures should be taken by teachers to use collaborative communication tools to promote interactions between higher vocational college English teachers and their students, and cooperation among the students, with focus on stimulating higher vocational college students' interest in learning, triggering their learning motivation, and giving more encouragement as well as timely and effective feedback to the students, so that higher vocational college students actively construct their own knowledge and understanding through their experiences, interactions, and reflections, enhance their English knowledge and develop their English language skills, especially their oral and written English skills.

2.3.2 Humanistic Learning Theory

The humanistic learning theory was developed by Abraham Maslow, Carl Rogers, and James F. T. Bugental in the early 1900's. The important principles involved in the humanistic learning theory are listed as follows:

（1）Attach importance to learner's choice. Learner's choice is central to the humanistic learning theory. It advocates that the learner enjoys freedom and autonomy to learn, which means that much of what a learner learns and how he or she learns is based on his or her own choice, not on the instructor's preferences. The learners can make choices ranging from daily activities to future goals.

（2）Put emphasis on learner's self-evaluation. Learner's self-evaluation is the most meaningful way to evaluate how a learners learning is progressing. It means that learners are responsible for evaluating their own advancement. When evaluation is based on a grading system, learners are encouraged to strive hard for a high grade rather than being passionate about what they are learning. In accordance with the humanistic learning theory, rote memorization and routine testing do not facilitate learning. In contrast, self-evaluation allows learners to experience satisfaction and excitement about what they have achieved. Learners will concentrate on improving themselves based on the standards they have set.

（3）Foster engagement to inspire learners to become self-motivated to learn. In accordance with the humanistic learning theory, learners all have intrinsic desires to become their best selves, which means that learners need to be involved in the learning process. The desire to learn should come from the learners. That's to say, instructors need to foster learners' curiosity and encourage them to pursue their interests. Once motivated by instructors, learners will become active participants in the learning process and develop a passion for learning.

（4）Feelings and knowledge are both important to the learning process and should not be separated. Humanistic learning theory advocates that knowledge and feelings are closely intertwined in the learning process. Cognitive and affective learning are both important to humanistic learning. Lessons and activities should center on the entire student along with their intellect and feelings, not one or the other.

（5）Create a safe learning environment. Since humanistic learning centers on the entire student, it is crucial that instructors create a safe environment so that learners can have as many of their needs met as possible. The learners need to feel safe physically, mentally, and emotionally in order to be capable of concentrating on their learning. Therefore, instructors should be passionate about the idea of assisting students in meeting as many of their needs as possible.

The major implications of applying the Humanistic learning theory in the construction of high-quality vocational college English courses are listed below:

（1）Teach higher vocational college students English-language learning skills. Since learning is student-centered, the role of the higher vocational college English teachers is to be a facilitator and model. The teachers are responsible for helping higher vocational college students develop English-language learning skills, especially basic language skills, feel motivated and engaged, and provide them with different topics, materials, and tasks to choose from.

（2）Provide higher vocational college students motivation for classroom tasks. Humanistic learning focuses on engagement, so higher vocational college English teachers need to provide motivation and exciting activities to help higher vocational college students feel engaged about English learning. For example, employ gamification to increase students' engagement and motivation in English learning. Instead of prizes, students go up levels and earn experience points. This can help promote a student's intrinsic desire for improvement. Additionally, levels and experience points make it more convenient for students to evaluate their progress. Furthermore, this can help them develop a passion for English learning.

（3）Provide higher vocational college students different learning opportunities that cater to their interests and learning styles. For instance, students can choose to complete practical activities, watch videos, carry out research on the web, and/or take part in online discussions such as social media interaction and online forums etc.

（4）Give higher vocational college students flexibility in their schedules and modes of participation. Some higher vocational college students learn better in the morning, whereas others learn more efficiently later in the day. Some may want to join an online class, while others prefer to undertake their online lessons independently. Higher vocational college English teachers can look for and apply adaptive software or applications or platforms that enable students' independent and self-paced study.

（5）Create opportunities for higher vocational college students' group work with peers. As a facilitator in the classroom, higher vocational college English teachers should create group opportunities to help students in higher vocational colleges explore, observe, and self-evaluate their own progress. They can perform this task better as they interact with other students who are learning concurrently.

2.3.3　Connectivism Learning Theory

Connectivism learning theory is an innovative approach to learning. It proposes that for effective learning, students should embrace the integration of thoughts, theories, and information they experience while using modern technology. It highlights the crucial role of digital tools in modern education, with recognition that the era of connectivity provides unlimited opportunities to shape our learning journeys. An intrinsic characteristic of connectivism is the promotion of group dynamics. Collaboration and open dialogue enables learners to benefit from diverse viewpoints, which can enhance decision-making, problem-solving, and the understanding of complex concepts. Furthermore, the connectivism learning theory supports the concept of decentralized learning, advocating the belief that real-time education is not confined to an individual but extends beyond, covering platforms such as social media, online communities, and extensive informational databases. Md. Afroz Alam (2023) argues that connectivism learning theory assumes that learning is a process of making connections between concepts, ideas and experiences, and that these connections are facilitated by technology and social networks.

Connectivism learning theory employs the concepts of "nodes" and "links" by drawing inspiration from network theory, framing them as integral elements in explaining the learning process in our digital era. In this context, a node, is essentially any point or source of information, which can cover a range of entities such as people, organizations, databases, or other resources which can generate or process information. For instance, a node can be a professional with unique expertise, a library, or a social media community centered on a specific discussion topic. while links act as the bridges or relationships binding these nodes. They are the routes via which information traverses from one node to another. These links can manifest in various forms. For instance, it can be through mutual discussions, academic references, digital hyperlinks, or even social ties on networking sites.

Connectivism lays emphasis on the complex relationship between nodes and links. By drawing upon some established educational theories and contrasting with others, it proposes that knowledge is not centralized but rather distributed across an expansive network of connections. Contrary to many older educational theories regarding students simply as passive recipients of knowledge, connectivism assumes that learning is shaped by the distribution of knowledge across networks and the interplay of connections within them.

Connectivism presents a modern shift in educational approaches, setting itself apart from the traditional classroom setting. It advocates that the responsibility of learning does not lie solely with the teacher. Rather, learners play a more central role in their own educational journey. Students are no longer regarded as passive recipients of knowledge; they are actively accountable for their own learning and personal growth, which constitutes a notable departure from some conventional methods and theories such as constructivism or cognitivism. In a connectivist classroom, the teacher shoulders a guiding role, directing students towards becoming effective navigators of their learning experiences. This is a dynamic process requiring students to make decisions and continuously expand their learning networks. The teacher plays the role of a coach or mentor, offering tools and guidance, while the learner takes on the role of the explorer, discovering new paths and developing new connections.

Connectivism brings numerous benefits for both students and teachers. Some of the most important merits are listed as follows:

（1）Collaboration. Connectivism puts emphasis on learning as a process where students refine new ideas based on their pre-existing knowledge. Through promoting active learning and problem-solving, it can encourage students to work collaboratively. In these circumstances, students can share and challenge each other's viewpoints, resulting in deeper understanding and jointly developed knowledge.

（2）Empowerment. Connectivism places students at the centre of the learning process, enabling them to actively engage with and build upon their knowledge, which can empower students by granting them control over their learning and fostering critical thinking. For teachers, connectivism shifts their role from being the providers of information to the facilitators of learning, allowing them to guide students actively and effectively in their learning journeys.

（3）Diversity. Connectivism advocates that each student brings their distinct prior knowledge and experiences to the connectivist learning environment. Through enabling students to build upon their own backgrounds and perspectives, connectivism honors this diversity. This approach can create an inclusive classroom atmosphere where diverse viewpoints are shared and integrated, resulting in more comprehensive understanding for all participants.

The major implications of applying the connectivism learning theory in the construction of high-quality vocational college English courses are listed below:

（1）Modify teaching methods to satisfy higher vocational college students' needs. There is a notable shift in the newest generation of learners who have grown up surrounded by technology, finding social media and collaborative tools integral to their daily lives. With recognition of this, higher vocational college English teachers should modify their teaching methods to mirror this technology-oriented learning process. For example, taking into consideration that a considerable portion of college students now source information from social media platforms, integrating these into the learning process of higher vocational college English can bridge the gap between traditional and modern learning techniques.

（2）Introduce flexible learning strategies to enhance the higher vocational college students' learning experience. A typical example is the concept of "drop-in" face-to-face study sessions led by instructors. While such sessions offer invaluable insights for some vocational college students, they might not be desired by all students. Therefore, through providing higher vocational college students the liberty to choose their participation, teachers can cater to both those who thrive in group settings and also independent learners. In addition, higher vocational college English teachers might go further and incorporate hybrid learning, with an English teacher or instructor delivering materials to learners, some of whom attend class in person, while others join the class virtually from home.

（3）Be better prepared for teaching content. In terms of teaching content of higher vocational college English, it is crucial for English teachers to evaluate their lesson plans based on the core principles of connectivism. Higher vocational college English teachers should consistently assess whether their teaching content is practical, relevant, and encourages interaction both between students and between students and technology. A practical project that requires higher vocational college students to collaborate and make use of various online resources could serve as a positive example of content that meets these criteria.

（4）Organize a variety of activities to encourages higher vocational college students to actively engage in English learning. It is important to note that the essence of connectivism is not restricted to the digital realm. Even in the absence of technology, its principles can find a place in the traditional classroom setting. Through activities such as group projects and open-ended discussions, the role of the higher vocational college English teacher subtly transforms from being the primary source of information to a guiding force. It encourages higher vocational college students to actively participate, challenge assumptions, and collaboratively arrive at conclusions, ensuring a more holistic and interactive learning journey and more satisfactory learning outcomes.

2.3.4   Mastery Learning Theory

Mastery learning theory, also referred to as learning for mastery theory, is a learning theory that shifts the definition of student's aptitude. In the traditional learning theory, content is taught within a fixed period of time, and students' aptitudes are based on how much they learned during that period. According to mastery learning theory, students' aptitudes are based on how long they need to master the content. It is assumed that all students, when given sufficient time and intervention, can ultimately master the content. The mastery learning theory aims to ensure that students truly master each course's subject material before they move on to the next course. For instance, if a student is learning a complicated language grammar point, according to mastery learning theory, they would not be rushed to move on until they have fully understood and can apply that grammar rule correctly. This approach contrasts with traditional learning theory in which students might move forward regardless of their level of mastery.

The works of mastery learning model typically involves five stages: pre-assessment, instruction, formative assessment, correction or enrichment instruction, and summative grading or assessment.

1. Pre-Assessment

At the very beginning, a teacher will introduce course material that are related to the standards they are required to teach via a pre-assessment. Its purpose is to ensure that students have previously mastered the necessary skills or knowledge before progressing to the current material. If the students lack the necessary competencies, the teacher will go backward to ensure that students have mastered the previous material before they move forward.

2. Instruction

Once students have displayed competency in the foundational skills or knowledge which are necessary for them to learn the current material, the teacher will begin to give instructions. It is essential that teachers have a clear communication of the mastery grading scale which they will use to determine whether the students have achieved the level of competency.

3. Formative assessment

Following the instruction stage, teachers will make an assessment of students' skills and knowledge by means of formative assessment. Formative assessment is capable of measuring students' competencies through a diverse range of methods, such as exit tickets, homework assignments, and classroom polls.

4. Correction or enrichment instruction

Once teachers make a judgement of where students are in the mastery process, they can provide differentiated instructions as needed. Students who display a high level of competency can continue to expand their knowledge and develop their skill set through personalized enrichment instruction which often occurs in small groups, while those who have not demonstrated the necessary mastery can receive extra personalized instruction and practice opportunities from the teacher. For example, in an English language class, proficient students can engage in advanced writing tasks or discussions in small groups, while those needing more support can receive individualized grammar lessons and additional writing practice with the teacher's guidance.

5. Summative assessment

The summative assessment is the final step in the learning process. Once a teacher believes that all students are at or close to "master" level, they provide cumulative tests, essays, or projects to assess whether students have mastered the content.

There are three major benefits of mastery learning model. To above all, mastery learning model sets students up to succeed. Mastery learning model focuses on every student and his or her learning journey toward growth, and ideally, mastery. It offers students as much time and intervention as necessary, enabling each student to be well-prepared to advance to the next level. Studies have shown that the mastery learning model closes the gap among different levels of aptitude by offering slower learners ample time for learning, and providing faster learners with sufficient enrichment to keep them engaged with the material. Thus, every student can achieve success. Additionally, mastery learning model inspires student's love of learning for the sake of learning. The shift from aptitude based on ability to aptitude based on time moves the weight of perceived intelligence off a student's shoulders. In the traditional learning model, students constantly strive to keep up and may potentially give up when they realize they have fallen behind. However, students in the mastery learning model come to understand that their aptitudes solely depend on their decision regarding the time and effort they need to put in learning the material. Grades are no longer a matter of competition; instead, each student works towards what is best for mastering the necessary content, allowing all students to progress together. Learning becomes much more collaborative, and it is often reported by teachers that students engaged in mastery learning start to explore the content out of their love for learning, rather than out of fear of poor grades. Last but not least, mastery learning model puts the responsibility for learning in the hands of the students. Since teachers shoulder the responsibilities of creating learning environments that foster students' individual learning needs to truly master the content, students begin to realize they must advocate for themselves when they don't understand something. Teachers often report an increase in students' motivation, sense of control over their education, and resilience as students find agency in navigating through their learning process. Students can no longer blame poor grades on bad teaching; instead, they are provided with as much time and as many opportunities as necessary until they master the content. They work hard with the teachers to understand any learning barriers until they find the paths that are suitable for them to achieve the best understanding and mastery of the content. A typical example in English-language learning context is that if a student struggles with grammar, he or she should take the initiative to practice more and ask for specific guidance from teachers to overcome the difficulty.

The major implications of applying the mastery learning theory in the construction of high-quality vocational college English courses are listed below: Different from "reteaching", mastery learning model provides vocational college students with as much time and intervention as needed to accommodate their different learning styles, modalities, and intelligence levels. In this circumstance, the higher vocational college English teachers should give differentiated and personalized instructions according to students' different levels of aptitude so that students can lessen the amount of time needed for remediation in the later units, enabling higher vocational college English teachers to cover just as much material as they would use traditional learning models. They also need to provide effective enrichment activities to learners who have mastered the material and do not need corrective instruction. With an aim to provide higher vocational college students challenging yet rewarding learning experiences, these activities should allow students to explore a greater depth of related topics that arouse their interests in learning. These enrichment activities could take the form of academic games and exercises, various multimedia projects, and peer discussions (Guskey, 2010). Since Bloom believes that as long as sufficient learning time and appropriate teaching are provided, almost all students can complete the corresponding teaching tasks. The gap between students with strong learning capability and those with weak learning capability lies in the length of time required to learn knowledge and develop skills. The online and offline hybrid learning mode used in the high-quality vocational college English courses is more consistent with the central idea of mastery learning. On the online platform, teachers can set up learning activities, paths and auxiliary cases to guide students to complete knowledge exploration on their own, giving students with weak learning capability the opportunity to shorten the gap with students with strong learning capabilities; the teachers can use the online platform to collect statistics and collect each student's learning situation, and provide timely feedback to students, supplemented by individual and personalized guidance, to teach students in accordance with their aptitude, effectively improve students' learning capabilities, and help higher vocational college students increase English knowledge, develop their English language skills.

2.4   Summary

From the above discussions, it can be concluded that the construction of higher vocational college English courses empowered by digitalization will be based on constructivism, humanism, connectivism, and mastery learning theories, focusing on student-centeredness, with teachers actively guiding, helping and promoting students to reconstruct the meaning of learning, making full use of various media teaching approaches and online teaching platforms, creating a scientific and effective online and traditional learning environment for learners, and realizing synchronous and asynchronous communication between teachers and students. It increases opportunities for discussions and practice and stimulates students' potential and interest in learning higher vocational college English, so as to meet students' needs for all-round development.

Chapter 3

Value and Connotation of High-quality Vocational College English Courses

3.1 Value of High-quality Vocational College English Courses

3.1.1 Upgrading Infrastructure to Offer Students Immersive, Interactive, and Personalized English Learning Experience

With the development and application of digital infrastructure, information networks, teaching equipment and facilities, online learning platforms, and innovative applications have become the foundation for digital transformation of higher vocational college English teaching and learning. As digital and intelligent technologies are integrated into vocational college English, teaching and learning of college English is undergoing profound changes, giving rise to a variety of teaching approaches and methods and providing college students with an immersive, interactive, and personalized English learning experience. It is very convenient for the vocational college English teachers to use AI for data collection, data analysis and presentation and application of the results of the students' English learning, and give personalized homework assignments to the college students according to their individual aptitudes. In this circumstance, the responsibility for English learning is put in the hands of the students by the vocational college English teachers. They play an active role in creating learning environments that foster higher vocational college students' individual learning needs to truly master the content. With the support of digital technology, the students are given as much time and as many opportunities as they need until they master the content. They work with the teachers to understand any learning blocks of higher vocational college English until they find the paths that work for them to best understand and master the content. What's more, the students begin to realize they must advocate for themselves when they don't understand something, leading to growth in students' motivation for and sense of control over their English learning, and resilience as students find agency in navigating through their vocational college English learning process.

3.1.2   Achieving Innovation in Teaching Philosophies, Approaches and Practices of Vocational College English

The integration of digital technology such as artificial intelligence, big data, and cloud computing into vocational college English, which has greatly improved the teaching environment, helps us transcend temporal and spatial boundaries of teaching and learning of vocational college English. The integration of online and offline teaching, and genuine and virtual realities makes higher vocational college students better learners. The inclusive, equitable, and high-quality supply and application of varied and rich digital resources, the combination of big data and statistical analysis, and the growing computing power have made teaching of vocational college English more targeted. Improvement of digital literacy and skills has contributed to teachers' competence. The combination of digital training for teachers, AI-based teaching assistants and AI teachers makes better teachers of vocational college English. They are encouraged to improve their digital literacy in aspects such as information awareness, computational thinking, mathematical learning and social responsibility, which enhance vocational college English teachers' awareness and capabilities in using digital technology to innovate their English language teaching activities. It allows for individualized and personalized instruction, as higher vocational college students can watch or listen to the pre-recorded lessons as many times as necessary to understand the content, pause or rewind to review difficult concepts and proceed when ready. As a result, class time can be utilized for more interactive activities such as collaborative projects, group discussions and hands-on experiments. This kind of practice promotes active learning and keeps higher vocational college students engaged. It fosters a learning environment where higher vocational college students can receive immediate feedback in classroom teaching activities. With higher vocational college English teachers freed from delivering standard lectures during class time, they can circulate among students to provide targeted assistance and address specific needs, which helps to build a good teacher-student relationship and personalize the students' English language learning.

3.1.3　Keeping a Record of the Whole Teaching Process and Facilitating the Implementation of Teaching Quality-assurance Measures

The transparency and traceability of teaching process and operation are the fundamental characteristics of high-quality vocational college English courses, which realize the transformation of traditional "gray box" teaching mode that is difficult to trace and monitor to the "white box" teaching mode that can keep a record of the whole teaching process. The advanced digital technology enables vocational college English teachers to trace and monitor the students' learning in real time through a variety of digital devices, giving the teachers accurate information about the students' learning at all times, which allows the teachers to set up learning activities, paths and auxiliary cases to guide students to complete knowledge exploration and skills development on their own. Additionally, the teaching documents such as professional talent training programs, higher vocational college English curriculum standards, teaching plans, and teaching progress tables are digitally stored in the teaching management platform and pushed to the personal space of teachers and students, which not only facilitates teachers to improve work efficiency, but also helps students to query professional learning goals, tasks and requirements online, and promote personalized learning, which not only helps to grow vocational college students' sense of responsibility, achievement, and participation, but also paves the way for the students to truly understand the content and embrace learning for the joy and challenge of learning. What's more, the course design, resource deployment and teaching arrangements, as well as the students' learning activities, all can leave running track "data" on the teaching platform, which is not only conducive to the diagnosis and improvement of teaching and learning by teachers and students, but also conducive to the quality control department of the academic affairs to carry out quality monitoring, thereby improving the quality of teaching and learning of higher vocational college English.

3.1.4   Promoting Innovation in Assessment and Evaluation Mechanisms and Achieving Comprehensive Management of Learning Quality

Technology-empowered assessment has been used for both summative and formative assessment activities in high-quality vocational college English courses. It is especially suitable for formative assessment purposes, since it provides mechanism for sharing immediate feedback, diagnosing and testing skills and knowledge, peer- and self-assessment, as well as offering private and non-judgmental feedback. Firstly, the frequency, content and methods of assessment and evaluation are innovative. The online teaching platform can quickly and conveniently test students' learning effects through pre-class tasks, in-class tests and after-class homework. By changing the staged and node-based assessments in the form of traditional mid-term and final written exams to comprehensive assessments of knowledge, skills and literacy and systematic assessments of digital in-class tests implemented through the teaching platform, the assessment can be transformed from learning effect testing to enhancing teaching and learning through assessment. Secondly, the course performance calculation method is innovative. By setting online learning performance evaluation rules, the learning participation (comprehensive scoring such as learning time, resource viewing rate, interactive participation rate, etc.), homework and test average scores, etc. are comprehensively taken into consideration to calculate the usual scores, and the students' learning efficiency and effects are objectively and systematically evaluated, which encourages students to actively learn and improve themselves. Thirdly, the students' learning status monitoring and management mechanism is innovative. The teachers use the online teaching platform and the school-based information service and decision support platform to conduct multi-dimensional process monitoring of students' online learning behaviors and results, analyze students' learning status through big data, and innovate students' academic monitoring mechanisms. It provides the vocational college English teachers with intelligent assessment tools that can compile test papers, evaluate objective questions and assist in the evaluation of subjective questions, while analyzing students' learning behavior data and guiding students according to their specific aptitudes and performances.

3.2　Connotation of High-quality Vocational College English Courses

3.2.1　Essence of High-quality Vocational College English Courses

The "high-quality course" proposed in the Notice of the Ministry of Education on Implementing the Spirit of the National Conference on Undergraduate Education in the New Era has the "two qualities and one degree" attributes of high-level, innovative and challenging. "High-quality course" is a quality requirement and value judgment for higher education courses, but the connotation of its quality standards is not clear. The newly revised Vocational Education Law, which came into effect on May 1st, 2022, has improved the recognition and status of vocational education by stressing it is as equally important as regular education. The implementation of the new law improves the status and attractiveness of vocational education. It requires governments at different levels to increase funding of vocational education and strengthen the management of teachers and students to create a better learning environment. As the advanced stage of the modern vocational education system with Chinese characteristics, higher vocational education is both advanced and professional. In the context of high-quality development, it should be based on the regional industrial chain, with majors (groups) as the carrier, and guided by promoting students' career development and high-level employment and entrepreneurship. By cultivating high-quality technical and skilled talents that meet the needs of the industry, the adaptability and attractiveness of vocational education should be enhanced. Therefore, building high-quality vocational college English courses empowered by digitalization is an action to improve the quality of higher vocational courses. The high-quality vocational college English courses should not only have the basic attributes of "two qualities and one degree", but also highlight the value standards of vocational education. That is to say, they should be able to organically integrate knowledge, abilities, and qualities that meet the needs of high-end industries, such as the new generation information technology, new energy, new materials, energy conservation & environmental protection, bio-medicine and health care, and cultivate students' comprehensive abilities to solve problems in application of technology in modern production and develop their innovative thinking; teaching content should be able to represent the new frontiers for the development of industrial technology and the mainstream of the times; teaching approaches and methods should be in line with the "Internet-based Education" environment, and can promote students' exploratory and personalized learning; vocational college English teachers need to spend time and energy on lesson planning and preparation, teaching, and pre- and after-class tutoring; students need to be engaged in deep learning, thinking, and cultivation to achieve the goal of constructing a course that is student-centered, teaching-based and outcome-oriented.

3.2.2 "Student-centered" Teaching Concept of High-quality Vocational College English Courses

The curriculum is the core element of talent cultivation, and its quality directly determines the quality of talent cultivation. It is also a concrete implementation of the fundamental task of "fostering virtue and nurturing talents", and the main purposes for teachers and students to work for and contribute to. With the continuous development of higher vocational education, the shortage of teachers has become a "common problem" in higher vocational colleges. Most teachers have no time to carry out scientific research, social services and seek self-improvement through training programs due to heavy teaching tasks. With the help of digital teaching resources and an integrated teaching and learning evaluation platform, through online auxiliary teaching or completely online teaching, it can effectively reduce the repetitive labor of higher vocational college English teachers in teaching, improve teaching quality and efficiency, enhance teachers' sense of satisfaction and achievement, and realize the comprehensive, balanced and personalized development of teachers. For students, courses are the main carrier of higher vocational college students' learning in campus, and "student-centered" is the key to curriculum implementation. High-quality vocational college English courses are conducive to changing students' superficial learning thinking of "hoping to teach test points in class and highlighting key points before the test". Through learning high-quality digital learning resources, a normalized learning environment is created where students can learn things at any time and any place, learn at their own pace, ask questions to and get answers from teachers and peers in case of need. Through online homework and self-tests, students' "burden" is appropriately "increased" to accomplish the goal of promoting learning through practice and achieving in-depth learning. It is necessary to change the traditional paper-based "one test determines the outcome" assessment method and transform it into a learning process assessment, give an assessment of students' academic performance more objectively, promote students' active and selective learning, meet students' personalized learning needs, and achieve the purpose of adding value to and empowering talent training.

3.2.3   Constitutive Elements of the High-quality Vocational College English Courses

There are five constitutive elements of the high-quality vocational college English courses: teachers, teaching materials, teaching and learning conditions, students, and evaluation and assessment. Firstly, teachers are the implementers and leading builders of high-quality vocational college English courses and are responsible for the quality of the courses. Therefore, teachers are required to have solid knowledge, rigorous teaching attitudes, advanced teaching concepts, enhanced digital literacy, and familiarity with the actual requirements of enterprises, and have the ability to implement modular teaching design and digital learning evaluation and assessment. They can skillfully use the online teaching platform to implement online teaching, attach importance to communication and interaction with students, and adapt their teaching strategies to student needs and help them develop efficient study habits. Secondly, with the support of modern digital technology, "high-quality courses" must change teaching materials into learning materials. It is necessary to design new loose-leaf textbooks, manuals, and new forms of digital teaching materials based on students' professional capabilities and comprehensive literacy, and to create systematic, serialized, and digital high-quality teaching resources that integrate knowledge, ability, quality, and skill training based on the principle of "learnable and easy to learn". Thirdly, good teaching and learning conditions are the guarantee for the implementation of high-quality vocational college English courses, including favorable classroom environments that can support digital teaching and learning, advantageous network conditions and tech-powered learning tools that support ubiquitous learning, and powerful and easy-to-operate online learning platforms. Fourthly, students are participants in building high-quality vocational college English courses, and their digital literacy, learning initiative, enthusiasm, self-discipline, and even ability for self-study, motivation for and interest in learning are closely related to the quality of vocational college English courses. Fifthly, the learning evaluation and assessment of high-quality vocational college English courses should adopt a combination of formative assessment and summative assessment, focusing on the evaluation of students' classroom attendance, participation in classroom activities, learning effectiveness and satisfaction. That is to say, the assessment is based on students' participation, achievement, improvement and development in their English language skills.

Chapter 4

Necessity and Feasibility of Construction of High-quality Vocational College English Courses Empowered by Digitalizatin

4.1 Necessity of Construction of High-quality Vocational College English Courses Empowered by Digitalization

4.1.1 Construction of High-quality Vocational College English Courses Empowered by Digitalization Is an Inevitable Trend to Embrace the Digital Age

Digital tools such as online teaching platforms, intelligent teaching systems, virtual reality (VR) and augmented reality (AR) technologies can provide students with richer and more intuitive learning materials and interactive experiences, making abstract language knowledge vivid and concrete, thereby stimulating students' interest in learning and improving learning efficiency. At the same time, these tools can also help teachers accurately analyze students' learning, realize personalized teaching, and further improve the quality of teaching. Traditional classroom teaching is restricted by both time and space, but digital teaching breaks down this barrier. Students can access learning resources anytime and anywhere through the web, allowing for self-directed and collaborative learning. This flexibility not only meets the diverse learning needs of students, but also provides them with more opportunities to practice and apply English. Digital technology has enabled high-quality teaching resources to be shared across geographical boundaries. Vocational colleges can introduce high-quality English course resources at home and abroad to enrich teaching content and improve teaching level by establishing a digital teaching resource library and participating in online course alliances. At the same time, teachers can also use the digital platforms to exchange experience and conduct teaching research, and jointly promote the building of high-quality vocational college English courses with more attention given to cultivating students' practical English-language competence and cross-cultural communication ability, so that they can better adapt to the needs of the workplace in the future.

4.1.2   Construction of High-quality Vocational College English Courses Empowered by Digitalization Is an Essential Requirement for Deepening the Reform of "Three Teachings"

Digitalization empowers the building of public English courses in higher vocational colleges, which requires teachers not only to have solid English language skills, but also to master modern information technology, such as multimedia teaching, online teaching platform operation, big data analysis, etc. Teachers need to transform from traditional knowledge transmitters to learning facilitators, resource integrators and technology applicators. Through digital means, teachers can design teaching activities more flexibly and guide students' learning in a personalized way, thereby improving teaching effectiveness. The building of high-quality vocational college English courses should make full use of digital resources, such as online courses, virtual simulation experiments, multimedia materials, etc., so that the teaching content is closer to the actual situation of the workplace and meets the personalized learning needs of students. Digital technology offers endless possibilities for innovative teaching methods. Teachers can adopt new teaching modes such as flipped classrooms, blended learning, and project-based learning, and make full use of online and offline resources to stimulate students' interest in learning and improve their self-directed learning ability. At the same time, through digital means of classroom interaction, real-time feedback and evaluation, we can have a more comprehensive understanding of students' learning and adjust teaching strategies in a timely manner. To sum up, building high-quality vocational college English courses empowered by digitalization is an essential requirement for deepening the reform of the "three teachings". It not only helps to improve teachers' teaching capabilities, enrich the content of teaching materials, and innovate teaching methods, but also promotes educational equity and resource sharing, and provides strong support for cultivating high-quality skilled talents with international mindset, practical English-language competence and cross-cultural communication skills.

4.1.3 Construction of High-quality Vocational College English Courses Empowered by Digitalization Is an Inevitable Choice to Improve the Teaching Effect of the Course

The development and application of modern digital technology enables the higher vocational college English teachers to improve the quality of higher vocational college English through modernizing traditional classroom teaching and learning and making high-quality teaching resources more accessible to all English learners in higher vocational colleges. Digitalization makes higher vocational college students' English learning much more personal,adaptive, interactive and enjoyable. When the students learn English on a computer or electronic terminals, the computer or electronic terminals can figure out how they study and then adapt their learning correspondingly. Supported by augmented reality, digitalization can offer higher vocational college students opportunities, practice and experience unseen before, and can create infinite new learning modes to make the students more energized and improve their participation in learning higher vocational college English. Based on their profiles, interests, skills, capabilities and aspirations, the higher vocational college English teachers can recommend tailor-made content to students, monitor their progress, give feedback and adjust teaching modes and methods based on the students' professional development. Building high-quality vocational college English courses empowered by digitalization is an important way to adapt to the trend of digitalizaiton, improve the teaching effect of the course, and promote the high-quality development of English-language learning of higher vocational college students of non-English majors.

4.2   Feasibility of Construction of High-quality Vocational College English Courses Empowered by Digitalization

The report of the 20th CPC National Congress pointed out that "we will promote the digitalization of education and build a society and country of learning where lifelong learning is pursued by all". Digitalization of education is a very special stage of educational informatization, which specifically refers to the process of continuously using digital, networked and intelligent technical means to transform the education and teaching system. Digitalization not only refers to digital technologies and tools, but also a systematic project of transformation of ideas and behavioral patterns. Digital technologies have injected new impetus into the building of high-quality vocational college English courses. Building high-quality vocational college English courses with digital empowerment can enrich the teaching content, cater to the needs of learners, innovate the teaching modes and assist in teaching evaluations and assessments.

4.2.1   Enriching the Teaching Content of High-quality Vocational College English Courses Empowered by Digitalization

With the development and application of digital technologies represented by big data, cloud computing, blockchain, artificial intelligence, and the Internet of things, knowledge sharing and Internet teaching have gradually become popular. As a result, digital resources with diverse types and rich content have been generated, which are quickly disseminated and convenient to use. On one hand, through the in-depth integration of the teaching resources of higher vocational college English with adoption of digital technologies, the establishment of a comprehensive, three-dimensional, high-quality digital resource library can enrich the teaching content of higher vocational college English, thereby providing higher vocational college English teachers with massive learning resources, teaching case libraries, key and difficult teaching points libraries, online demonstration course libraries etc., to help higher vocational college English teachers to explain the knowledge deeply, thoroughly and vividly. When vocational college English teachers make good use of digital resources, they can make the teaching of higher vocational college English more lively, expand the classroom platform and broaden the students' horizons.

4.2.2 Innovating the Teaching Modes of High-quality Vocational College English Courses Empowered by Digitalization

Continuously innovating teaching modes is an important way to enhance the attractiveness and appeal of higher vocational college English in the new era. Digital technology empowers the building of high-quality vocational college English courses, further promotes the transformation of its teaching modes, and improves the head-up rate and nodding rate of higher vocational college English. Firstly, it promotes the digital transformation of teaching modes. Through flipped classrooms, online and offline mixed learning, pre-class micro-module and other methods, the digitalization of classroom, teaching designs, teacher-student interactions and so on have been promoted, and the innovative expression and scenario-based narration of higher vocational college English courses have been promoted. It not only improves the classroom participation of higher vocational college students, but also fully mobilizes the autonomy of students' thinking. Secondly, it promotes the digital transformation of students' learning methods. The application of digital technologies such as VR technology, artificial intelligence, big data analysis and so on, facilitates the building of interactive learning center giving students a personalized immersive experience in higher vocational college English, allowing the students to fully experience the fun of experiential and immersive classrooms, strengthen the students' emotional experience, and fully improve students' classroom participation and interest in learning.

4.2.3　Assisting in Teaching Evaluations and Assessments of High-quality Vocational College English Courses Empowered by Digitalization

How to evaluate the teaching effect of higher vocational college English comprehensively, objectively and accurately is the final step of the teaching process of high-quality vocational college English course. Traditionally, the teaching effect of higher vocational college English is generally evaluated by students' evaluation and experts' assessment. There are inevitably some disadvantages, such as a strong subjective intention, inability to achieve dynamic tracking and real-time feedback. The development and application of digital technology offers new possibilities for accurately evaluating the teaching effect of higher vocational college English. On one hand, digital technology can realize the digitization, indexing and explicitness of the teaching evaluation of higher vocational college English with its super computing power, strong storage technology, big data and AI analysis capabilities, establish an accurate and clear monitoring and evaluation mechanism, and make the teaching evaluations more scientific and diverse. On the other hand, digital technology can dynamically record the specific situation of teachers' "teaching" and students' "learning", and provide more scientific and efficient teaching feedback and evaluation of higher vocational college English. At the same time, digital technology can give objective analysis of the collected feedback data, find loopholes in the teaching process, and screen the factors that are not conducive to the teaching of higher vocational college English, so as to help English teachers in higher vocational colleges improve the teaching effect of higher vocational college English and adjust teaching methods in time. The adoption of digital technology to construct a comprehensive evaluation system for teaching of higher vocational college English will help to create high-quality higher vocational college English that are confident, down-to-earth, popular and vibrant, making the courses attractive and the classrooms lively, allowing students to learn English actively, happily and efficiently, and improve their English learning outcomes.

4.2.4 Catering to the Needs of Learners of High-quality Vocational College English Courses Empowered by Digitalization

Catering to the needs of learners is an inherent requirement for boosting the pertinence and effectiveness of higher vocational college English. Digitalization empowers the building of higher vocational college English courses, which can have a better understanding of the personality characteristics, learning habits, learning strengths, knowledge gaps, etc. of the higher vocational college students, and learn about their wants and needs. Firstly, digital technologies such as big data, artificial intelligence, and cloud computing can accurately portray the learning behavior of the higher vocational college students, capture the data of the learners such as the learners' attention to specific knowledge, classroom concentration, and emotional changes. Meanwhile, more personalized teaching and guidance can be provided according to the learners' learning habits, preferences and characteristics, forming personalized knowledge maps, and truly teaching students in accordance with their individuality and aptitudes. Secondly, digitalization can promote the construction of a personalized lifelong learning system. The digital learning platforms, conducive to the opening and sharing of quality teaching resources of

higher vocational college English, can make higher vocational college students'
learning modes more flexible, learning resources more abundant, and learning
terminals more popular, so that higher vocational college students can learn
English at any time and any place.

Chapter 5

Status Quo and Countermeasures of Construction of High-quality Vocational College English Courses Empowered by Digitalization

5.1 Problems in Construction of High-quality Vocational College English Courses Empowered by Digitalization

5.1.1 Conceptual Dilemma: Teachers and Students' Insufficient Digital Awareness and Thinking

The building of high-quality vocational college English courses requires not only advanced digital technological facilities, but also the change of the teachers' and students' thinking. Developing digital thinking is the premise and foundation for promoting the building of high-quality vocational college English courses. However, judging from the current situation, during the construction of high-quality vocational college English courses with digitalization empowerment, teachers and students generally do not have a deep understanding of digitalization, fail to develop a scientific understanding of digital transformation, and even have misunderstandings to varying degrees. Firstly, some higher vocational college English teachers and students are not familiar with and master the relevant knowledge and skills of teaching reform of higher vocational college English empowered by digitalization. And their sensitivity to, acceptance of and approval of the construction of high-quality vocational college English courses empowered by digitalization are insufficient. Secondly, some higher vocational college English teachers and students deem the building of high-quality vocational college English courses empowered by digitalization with the information-based teaching of higher vocational college English. They believe that the building of high-quality vocational college English courses empowered by digitalization is simply the information-based teaching of the higher vocational college English. They think that the building of high-quality vocational college English courses empowered by digitalization has just transformed from offline to online. It is just a nickname for

information-based teaching of higher vocational college English in the new stage
of development. Thirdly, some higher vocational college English teachers and
students believe that the building of high-quality vocational college English
courses will only be carried out on a small scale and is a matter for a few "Double
Top" higher vocational colleges and has little to do with ordinary higher vocational
colleges. Fourthly, some teachers and students in higher vocational colleges are
afraid of difficulties and believe that the process of building high-quality
vocational college English courses empowered by digitalization is too complicated,
which will bring additional burdens of management costs to higher vocational
colleges and increase the burden on teachers and students. Fifthly, some higher
vocational college English teachers and students believe that building high-quality
vocational college English courses empowered by digitalization is only phased and
temporary and will not be carried out in a long-term and stable manner. These
misunderstandings and concepts have also hindered the construction of high-
quality vocational college English courses to a certain extent.

5.1.2   Facility Dilemma: Insufficient Digital Infrastructure and Equipment in Higher Vocational Colleges

Because the current digital transformation of education is still at the
preliminary stage, a complete digital technology ecosystem has not yet formed,
and the construction of digital technology infrastructure in some higher vocational
colleges is unfinished, which led to insufficient digital technology supply. In
addition, some higher vocational colleges still rely on information systems built in
the early stages of digital transformation, and most of these systems are not
compatible with multi-platform systems. Data resources cannot be shared,
interoperable, and integrated, ultimately leading to the dilemma of information
islands. The second is data management issues. Currently, the insufficient supply
of digital technology hinders information connectivity and data circulation to a
certain extent, and limits the use of digital technology in public English courses in
higher vocational colleges. Thirdly, some English teachers in higher vocational

colleges lack effective data analysis capabilities, so the behavioral data of some higher vocational college English teachers cannot be fully collected and applied. Furthermore, some digital technology suppliers cannot meet the individual needs of higher vocational college English teachers in different teaching scenarios. Most of them only provide general solutions, which ultimately results in the inability of data elements to play a driving role. Another big problem is data security issues. The construction of high-quality vocational college English courses will involve the storage of a large amount of data, including personal information of higher vocational college English teachers and students as well as teaching resources. These important information data need to be stored securely. Therefore, how to ensure data security is also an urgent issue that needs to be solved in building high-quality vocational college English courses.

5.1.3 Application Dilemma: Insufficient Digital Literacy and Skills of Teachers and Students

Teachers are the implementers of teaching and education and are the key to improving teaching quality. Judging from the current source of English teachers in higher vocational colleges, they are mainly fresh graduates from colleges and universities and personnel with industry and enterprise experience. Fresh graduates from colleges and universities have good educational backgrounds, but lack practical experience, and are good at theoretical teaching in the process of organizing teaching activities; while personnel with practical industry and enterprise experience have rich production and management skills and can teach based on their accumulated rich experience, but have weak theoretical literacy and insufficient teaching design capabilities. The problems of solidified sources and inert structure of teachers are manifested in teachers' lack of platform thinking to integrate resources and the innovative teaching design capabilities. In the digital era where digital technology is widely used in the teaching and educational process, the teaching environment has expanded from physical space to cyberspace, forming a personalized, ubiquitous, and intelligent dual-space teaching environment in which people and technology are highly integrated; teaching goals emphasize comprehensive cultivation of students' knowledge, skills and qualities required by high-quality technical talents with skills; teaching methods attach more importance to the cultivation of students' independent learning capabilities, based on precise "teaching" and personalized "learning"; students have also transformed from passive information receptors and recipients to learners in the digital age, who play the role of researchers, collaborators and practitioners actively managing their own behaviors, methods and preferences; learning feedback uses multiple methods based on big data evaluation, focusing on the learning process and learning behaviors, promoting timely improvement of teaching and learning through intelligent analysis and diagnosis, etc. All these require higher vocational college English teachers to have high digital literacy and the ability to interact and collaborate with digital technology, make full use of theories and methods such as teaching technology, curriculum and instruction theory, information science, and science of learning, and based on the systematic view of digital transformation of education, from innovation of theoretical system, design of technical system and implementation of teaching plan with aims to develop a new model of talents cultivation and a new mode of vocational college English teaching.

5.2　Causes of the Problems in Construction of High-quality Vocational College English Courses Empowered by Digitalization

5.2.1　Weak Digital Competence Hindering the Construction of High-quality Vocational College English Courses Due to the "Digital Divide"

In 2017, the Professional Digital Competence Framework for Teachers released by the Norwegian Centre for ICT in Education in 2017 pointed out that "to cultivate students who are adaptable to the digital age, professional digital competence must be regarded as an integral part of teacher competence and the teaching profession". In the future, digital technology will be more comprehensively applied to the teaching field of higher vocational colleges. As implementers of teaching technology, teachers urgently need to improve their digital competence to meet the increasingly dynamic and digital teaching needs. However, there are still many deficiencies in the digital literacy of public English teachers in higher vocational colleges. The rapid development of digital technology has forced higher vocational public English teachers to assume the role of organizers and implementers of information-based teaching as soon as possible, while higher vocational public English teachers who grew up in a traditional academic environment generally have insufficient competence to use digital technology. Some higher vocational public English teachers only have a simple grasp of educational technology and lack systematic learning of deeper educational technology. Of course, one reason is that the heavy teaching and scientific research tasks prevent them from paying attention to information-based teaching technology, but the more important reason is the lack of motivation for improvement. Moreover, there are significant differences in the level of digital competence among teachers from different higher vocational colleges, as well as teachers of different ages and genders, and the complexity of digital technology has also exacerbated the emergence of this phenomenon. Some higher vocational college English teachers have a superficial understanding of information-based teaching and are not aware of the individual responsibilities of teachers in the context of the development of information-based vocational education. They believe that information-based teaching is just about mastering basic computer-assisted teaching applications and being able to use audios, videos, images, PPT or some online teaching platforms. Their awareness of innovative teaching using digital technology is still relatively weak.

Whether digital technology can be effectively applied in the field of public English teaching in higher vocational colleges and whether it can truly improve the quality of public English teaching in higher vocational colleges depends on the public English teachers in higher vocational colleges. Their awareness and attitude towards digital technology determine whether they can truly bring into full play the empowerment of digital technology. Some public English teachers in higher vocational colleges tend to view the digital teaching reform in the field of vocational education with a negative attitude due to the coverage of instrumental rationality, which leads to the continuous elimination of the main role of public English teachers in the process of improving digital literacy. Some public English teachers in higher vocational colleges often think that they are not competent for this kind of teaching work, have great resistance, and even refuse digital teaching resources, exclude themselves from digital teaching, lack self-evaluation and reflection on digital teaching, and cannot fully see the positive role that digital technology brings to public English teaching in higher vocational colleges, which exacerbates digital bias. In addition, public English teachers in higher vocational colleges have relatively limited knowledge of digital information and digital ethics. Digital information is mainly due to the popularity of smart phones and computers, while digital ethics mainly comes from the inculcation of social software rules. However, since they mainly rely on smart tools to obtain relevant knowledge of fragmented digital technology and information, the knowledge is not systematic enough, so there is a clear lack of capability and literacy in digital technology.

5.2.2 Inadequate Digital Infrastructure Hindering the Construction of High-quality Vocational College English Courses Due to the "Infrastructure Defects"

Information itself is interconnected and interacts with living organisms and the surrounding environment to form a complete information ecosystem. Persons, behaviors, values and technology interact with each other in the same environment.

Its core is the persons served by technology, not technology. As an information ecological environment, the smart campus can provide a digital environment for the building of high-quality vocational college English courses. The campus is an important information ecological space for the building of high-quality vocational college English courses. The smart and digital campus with complete facilities plays an important role in promoting the building of high-quality vocational college English courses.

In July 2021, six departments including the Ministry of Education jointly issued the Guiding Opinions on Promoting the Construction of New Education Infrastructure and Building a High-Quality Education Support System, which pointed out that "Educational information infrastructure is guided by the new development concept, dominated by informationization, and built to serve the needs of high-quality development of education. It focuses on information networks, platform systems, digital resources, smart campuses, innovative applications, trusted security and other aspects of new infrastructure systems". Colleges and universities are encouraged to upgrade their technology, promote the integrated construction of campus physical space and cyberspace, and realize the intelligence and digitalization of teaching facilities, scientific research facilities and public facilities.

However, the current level of smart campus facilities construction in some higher vocational colleges is still unable to meet the needs of the construction of high-quality English courses in higher vocational colleges. Digital teaching activities using simulation software, VR and other information-based teaching technologies as training equipment have been launched in some higher vocational colleges, but the current number of training equipment has not yet met the needs of simulation teaching and cannot fully meet teachers' learning and application of digital technology. Full 5G network coverage can be achieved in higher vocational colleges, but there is room for improvement in network security protection capabilities and network security infrastructure construction. The construction of smart campuses in some higher vocational colleges is still at the stage of "giving more importance to hardware and less importance to software". Some vocational colleges have met the hardware equipment requirements but have neglected the full use of data information and lack effective software development, which has a certain negative impact on the subsequent upgrade and application of smart campuses.

5.2.3　Imperfect Incentive Mechanism Hindering the Construction of High-quality Vocational College English Courses Due to the "Management Gap"

In the 1960s, American psychologist David C. Mc Clelland proposed the Achievement Motivation Theory. He believes that many human needs and motivations are not completely physiological, but are social and can be cultivated and stimulated. The construction of high-quality vocational college English courses is an ongoing process. Digital technology in higher vocational education is still at the preliminary stage. Teachers are prone to encounter difficulties and setbacks in the exploration. Some English teachers in higher vocational colleges have a weak awareness of lifelong learning and are not familiar with digital technology. The ignorance and passive acceptance of digital technology have seriously hindered the construction of public English courses in higher vocational colleges. Therefore, it is particularly important to implement the incentive mechanism of digital technology in school management. Developed countries generally attach great importance to the role of incentive mechanisms in curriculum construction, and provide sufficient financial support, training programs for teachers, paid leave and subsidies for teachers' participation in training, promotion and salary increase welfare etc. In China, a series of measures should be taken to fully mobilize the enthusiasm of teachers to participate in curriculum construction and reforms. A perfect incentive mechanism can invigorate teachers' enthusiasm and creativity in the construction of high-quality English courses in higher vocational colleges. Therefore, it is necessary to strengthen school management of encouraging teachers to leverage the role of digital technology in help then grading students' homework and English compositions, determining teaching rhythm, fostering greater interactivity with students and analyzing reports on students' classroom performance etc., especially stimulate higher vocational college English teachers' interest in continuously improving their curriculum construction capabilities and actively participating in the construction of high-quality courses.

5.3 Solutions to the Problems in Construction of High-quality Vocational College English Courses Empowered by Digitalization

5.3.1 Adopting Advanced Concepts of Construction of High-quality Vocational College English Courses Empowered by Digitalization

1. Adhering to the educational philosophy of "Fostering Virtue and Nurturing Talents"

The ultimate goal of curriculum construction must be attributed to the implementation of the fundamental task of "fostering virtue and nurturing talents", and the higher vocational college English teachers must firmly grasp the fundamental issues of "What kind of people we should cultivate, how, and for whom". This requires that curriculum construction must follow the laws of educational development, aim at and promote the all-round development of people, and can't just act as a carrier of objective knowledge. First of all, the English teachers in higher vocational colleges must pay attention to ideological issues, must integrate ideological and political education into curriculum construction. They must follow valuable advice that embodies the core socialist values and excellent traditional Chinese culture to guide curriculum construction, and use it as an effective carrier for cultivating the spirit of patriotism, spirit of professionals, the spirit of model workers, and the spirit of craftsmanship among students in higher vocational colleges. While paying attention to imparting students' knowledge and developing their abilities, we must also help students develop the correct outlook on the world, on life and on values. We must closely follow the tremendous changes in social forms, attach importance to cultivating talents needed for social progress, cultural heritage and national development. The higher vocational college English teachers should bear in mind their mission of cultivating talent for the Party and the country, developing teaching methods for the new era, and making more contributions to nurturing socialist builders and successors who have an all-round moral, intellectual, physical and aesthetic grounding with a hard-working spirit.

2. Adhering to the teaching concept of "student-centered"

Adhering to the teaching concept of "student-centered" and committed to helping higher vocational college students to grow up to become highly-skilled and capable of adapting to a rapidly changing work environment, vocational college English teachers can increase the controlability of the teaching process by leveraging the advantages of digital technologies such as the Internet of things, big data and artificial intelligence etc. The teachers can dynamically adjust the teaching materials and learning process based on students' cognitive ability and foundations of learning. Teachers can check the progress and effects of each student in real time. According to the feedback, teachers can change their ways of teaching and guidance, help students solve problems they encounter in time through interactive means, and target the best for students. Relying on digital technologies such as the Internet of things, big data and artificial intelligence etc., online education platforms are available for students to carry out online learning through computer terminals and mobile terminals. At the same time, it allows vocational college English teachers to comprehensively use pictures, audios, videos, interactive activities and other digital learning resources to enrich the classroom, enliven the classroom atmosphere and enable students to achieve effective teacher-student interaction and student-student interaction before, during and after class. With the help of big data, vocational college English teachers can analyze students' classroom behavior, learning effects and language skills, and making their English learning more individualized and effective. With the help of state-of-the-art technologies like AI and H5, the vocational college English teachers enable the students to experience the fun of learning English, enhance their interest and build up their self-confidence in learning English so students can continuously harvest learning results and make the progress to the greatest extent.

3. Adhering to the teaching concept of "striving for excellence through hard work and comprehensive learning"

The cultivation of "high-quality courses" is difficult to achieve overnight, and it requires the concentration of multiple resources such as human, financial and material resources and continuous and careful polishing. It must be admitted that the higher vocational college English teachers who can offer "high-quality courses" are by no means the majority, but a minority. They must be talented and knowledgeable person, be familiar with teaching strategies and methods, and of course have good eloquence and adaptability. At the same time, no matter how the course is positioned, "high-quality courses" must show excellent qualities in terms of content, ideas, and viewpoints, reflecting "content is king". Therefore, teachers in higher vocational colleges must earnestly shoulder the main responsibility for the construction of "high-quality courses", start with "changing themselves", improve their educational and teaching capabilities, scientific research abilities etc. Therefore, efforts should be made to provide training for higher vocational college English teachers with workshops and seminars, arrange on-site training for English teachers and administrative staff, make online classes available for teachers to develop their skills, and grant more funds for research and better equipment for vocational college English teaching.

5.3.2 Following the Reasonable Principles of Construction of High-quality Vocational College English Courses Empowered by Digitalization

1. Realizing integration of ideological and political education and the vocational college English teaching

In May 2020, the Ministry of Education issued the Guiding Outline of Curriculum Ideological and Political Construction in Colleges and Universities, which clearly requires all colleges and universities, all teachers, and all courses to undertake the responsibility of educating people, so that all kinds of courses and ideological and political courses can go hand in hand, unify explicit education and implicit education, form a synergistic effect, and build a general pattern of all-round education of all students. Exploring the internal relationship between the learning of basic language knowledge and skills and ideological and political education in curriculum teaching, integrating ideological and political education into vocational college English teaching, integrating value shaping, knowledge transmission and ability cultivation, and guiding students to shape a correct outlook on world, life, and values are what vocational college English teachers need to think deeply about and explore practice on.

As a compulsory course or restricted elective course for higher vocational college students, vocational college English course needs to keep up with the times, the vocational college English teachers needs to systematically understand and teach the latest progress and development both at home and abroad, and students need to establish strategic thinking to serve the country and contribute to the world, which requires the vocational college English course to do a good job in ideological and political education while keeping pace with the times and teaching and educating people. It is important for the vocational college English teachers to adopt effective strategies to realize the objective of political and ideological education in vocational college English courses and integrate the political and ideological education into the instruction of the English language, culture and thinking by making the best of the political and ideological resources in the textbooks now in use.

2. Realizing the integration of industry and education and school-enterprise cooperation in construction of high-quality vocational college English courses

Integration of industry and education, and school-enterprise cooperation are the source of higher vocational education. In the process of digital empowering the construction of high-quality vocational college English courses, higher vocational colleges should closely cooperate with universities, research institutes and leading businesses. Firstly, we must "go out" and send vocational college English teachers to businesses to deepen their understanding of the development trends of the industry and enterprises and the latest technology and standards for specific industries, strengthen the connection between higher vocational public English course teaching and the real needs in real working scenarios and build up students' capabilities to meet those needs. Secondly, we must "bring in" and recruit skilled craftsmen, industry experts, and highly skilled talents in the industry to build a strong teaching team composed of full-time and part-time teachers with rich teaching and practical experiences, jointly participate in the formulation of curriculum standards and teaching plans, regularly hold course construction seminars, and guide the construction of high-quality vocational college English courses. Efforts should be made to actively explore new models for the integration of industry and education sectors. With the support of digital technology, the industry's new technologies and new processes need to be presented to learners at a faster pace and in a more effective way.

3. Adhering to the principle of making English language learning serve the practical purpose in construction of high-quality vocational college English courses

Mr. Huang Yanpei has a clear positioning of vocational education, namely preparation for individuals to make a living, preparation for individuals to serve society, and preparation for increasing productivity for the country and the world. The higher vocational college English should fully reflect the principle of making English language learning serve the practical purpose, so that students can directly apply the knowledge and skills they have acquired to their jobs after learning, improve their practical problem-solving capacity, improve their workplace competence, enhance their professional development ability and social adaptability. That's to say, it is imperative for higher vocational college English teachers to impart "enough knowledge, effective methods, and practical skills" to students, adjust the structural employment contradictions of "difficulty in recruiting" and "difficulty in finding a job" and boost social recognition of vocational education. Therefore, for higher vocational education, not only high-level, innovative and challenging courses can be "high-quality courses". We must clear up misunderstandings, focus on improving training quality, and promote changes in teaching content and methods. Teachers in higher vocational colleges should have the idea of using their unremitted efforts to benefit students and be committed to exploring new models of talent cultivation and new ways of curriculum reform in higher vocational college English in the new era, optimizing their teaching design, developing rich teaching materials and innovating their teaching methods to improve the quality of higher vocational college English teaching.

4. Leveraging the role of digital technology in construction of high-quality vocational college English courses

Digital technology, with its unique advantages, provides a strong driving force and important support for the construction of high-quality vocational college English courses. It is very important for vocational college English teachers to possess the digital competence to guide learning work in a digital environment. This involves understanding and managing how this environment is constantly changing, and challenging the roles of the teachers. It is also imperative for the vocational college English teachers to make full use of the opportunities inherent in digital resources so as to develop a constructive and inclusive learning environment, and to adapt their teaching models to satisfy the demands of diverse groups of students in higher vocational colleges to interact and collaborate with technology. The teachers are also required to use diverse forms of assessment of students' learning in a digital environment, in ways that contribute to fostering their desire to learn, learning strategies and learning competence. The teachers also should get a clear understanding of how digital technology, digital teaching materials, and digital learning resources can help to motivate and support the higher vocational college students' learning processes. It is also important for vocational college English teachers to make great efforts to explore innovative teaching models empowered by digital technology to enrich the classroom activities, stimulate students' interest in learning English, increase their participation degree and sense of accomplishment, and realize the substantial reform of English teaching and learning in higher vocational colleges.

5.3.3   Utilizing Effective Methods of Construction of High-quality Vocational College English Courses Empowered by Digitalization

1. Accurately setting teaching objectives

Teaching objectives are not only an important part of the teaching process, but also one of the key factors in promoting the development of students. Accurately setting the teaching objectives of high-quality vocational college English courses can cater to the needs of higher vocational college students, effectively stimulate their interest and motivation in learning, and thus promote all-round development of students. Having an understanding of students' learning background and interests is an important prerequisite for accurately setting teaching objectives. Higher vocational college English teachers can have a better understanding of students' interests, learning needs and learning styles by leveraging the advantages of digital technology represented by big data, artificial intelligence, blockchain and 5G, thereby providing a basis for accurately setting teaching objectives. In addition, students' learning ability and potential are important factors for accurately setting teaching objectives. Vocational college English teachers can understand students' learning ability and potential through daily observation, test scores analysis, homework completion, etc., so as to formulate teaching objectives that meet the actual needs of students at different learning levels.

In the digital era, vocational college English teachers have an array of powerful digitally enabled tools at their disposal. For example, online learning platforms enable teachers to track students' daily learning behaviors in real-time through recording details such as the time students spend on each learning module, the frequency of their logins, and their participation in online discussions;

intelligent test score analysis software can help teachers deeply analyze students' test scores, which not only provides overall performance evaluations but also identifies specific areas where students struggle or excel; digital assignment platforms, which can automatically grade objective assignments and provide detailed feedback on subjective assignments, allow teachers to monitor students' progress in completing homework, identify patterns of procrastination or rushed work, and even analyze the time taken to complete different types of tasks. These digital means empower vocational college English teachers to develop three-dimensional learner profiles that transcend traditional observational limitations, which enables them to set teaching objectives that precisely meet the needs of students at different learning levels, ensuring that every student is challenged and supported appropriately in the learning process.

According to *English Curriculum Standards for Higher Vocational Education (2021 Edition)* released by the Ministry of Education in March 2021, the teaching objectives of vocational college English course is to fully implement the Party's education policy, cultivate and practice the core socialist values, implement the fundamental task of cultivating morality and educating people, and further promote the development of students' core English literacy, and cultivate high-quality technical and skilled talents with Chinese feelings and international vision who can communicate effectively in English in daily life and the workplace. Through the study of this course, students should be able to achieve the development goals of four core competencies of the English subject set by the curriculum standards.

（1）International communication in the workplace.

Students can master the necessary English phonetics, vocabulary, grammar, discourse and pragmatics knowledge, have the necessary English listening, speaking, reading, watching, writing and translation skills, be able to identify and use appropriate body language and multimedia means, use appropriate strategies according to the context, understand and express the meaning of oral and written words, and effectively complete communication tasks in daily life and workplace situations. Be good at listening and negotiating in communication, respect others, have empathy and sympathy; practice values such as patriotism, dedication, integrity, and friendliness.

（2）Multi-cultural communication.

Students can acquire knowledge of multiple cultures of the world through English learning, understand cultural connotations, incorporate cultural essence, foster a strong sense of community for the Chinese nation and a sense of community with a shared future for mankind, and develop the correct outlook on the world, on life and on values; to deepen the understanding of Chinese culture through cultural comparison, inherit traditional Chinese culture, and enhance cultural confidence; to adhere to the Chinese position, have an international perspective, be able to tell China's stories and spread Chinese culture in English; to master the necessary cross-cultural knowledge, have cross-cultural skills, uphold an equal, inclusive, and open attitude, and be able to effectively accomplish cross-cultural communication tasks.

（3）Improvement of linguistic thinking ability.

Through the analysis of oral and written English discourse, students can distinguish specific phenomena in language and culture, understand modes of thinking such as abstraction and generalization, analysis and synthesis, comparison and classification, distinguish the similarities and differences between Chinese and English modes of thinking, and have a certain level of logic, critical and innovative thinking, develop a habit of respecting facts, prudent judgment, fair evaluation, and good at exploration.

（4）Development of autonomous learning capabilities.

Students can understand the significance of English learning, establish a correct concept of English learning, have clear goals of English learning, be able to effectively plan learning time and learning tasks, use appropriate English learning strategies, formulate learning plans, select learning resources, monitor the learning process, and evaluate learning results. Students can adopt appropriate methods according to the needs of further studies and employment, and use English for lifelong learning.

2. Carefully developing teaching materials

Vocational college English teachers should pay close attention to alignment between job requirements and cultivation of higher vocational college students' knowledge and skills. Efforts should be made to integrate the new development of enterprises and industries into the development of teaching materials of vocational college English course, with top priority given to the development of innovative industries including advanced manufacturing, new energy, new materials, biotechnology and artificial intelligence. In addition, vocational college English teachers need to sort out the teaching materials according to the principle of "necessary and sufficient" and rely on digital technology to develop teaching materials with characteristics of practicality, flexibility, cutting-edge and challenging, so as to facilitate vocational English teachers to change their teaching concepts, innovate teaching models, diversify teaching methods, enrich teaching content. For example, in vocational college English courses for students majoring in Mechanical Engineering, VR-based teaching materials can be developed with the integration of artificial intelligence-powered virtual teaching assistants, enabling real-time human-machine interaction. Students can virtually step into a high-tech factory environment where they interact with virtual equipment, read English-labeled operation manuals, and communicate with virtual colleagues in English. This not only makes the learning experience more immersive but also directly aligns with the job requirements of the advanced manufacturing industry. The VR-based teaching materials should be updated regularly to contain the latest technology and standards for the manufacturing industry, such as new types of robotic arms or updated production line processes, which not only enhances teaching efficiency but also significantly boosts students' learning engagement. With the integrated mode, methods of higher vocational English teaching and learning become flexible and diverse, and the ways teaching activities are organized also are more flexible than in the past, which is conducive to teacher-student and student-student interaction in classroom teaching, and students are happy to think, learn, enjoy, and use what they have learned, so that classroom teaching can truly become the main channel and main battlefield for students to learn knowledge and cultivate abilities.

By leveraging the advantages of digital technology represented by big data, the Internet of things, cloud computing and artificial intelligence, the practical and flexible teaching materials of high-quality vocational college English courses provide uninterrupted learning support for English learners in higher vocational colleges, develop a comprehensive digital learning space with more intelligent and portable learning terminals, and construct a fully covered digital learning community for higher vocational college students to learn anytime, anywhere, without time and space constraints, productively and efficiently.

For example, in a higher vocational college English course related to introducing new materials, the employment of e-textbooks, with the advantage of being able to tie in with multimedia technology, can provide students with an effective and interactive learning experience. When students point their mobile devices at certain pages about new materials like graphene, AR pop-ups can show 3D models of the material's molecular structure, along with English explanations of its properties and applications. Teachers can further enrich these dynamic resources by embedding interactive knowledge checks, such as drag-and-drop molecular composition exercises, alongside hyperlinks to related industry reports from leading materials research journals. These digital teaching resources combine the necessary and sufficient knowledge and skills with a high degree of effectivenss and interactivity, making learning more engaging and relevant to the latest development in the industry.

It is very important for vocational college English teacher to locate, critically evaluate, choose, and integrate digital teaching materials and digital learning resources of vocational college English based on pedagogical, English didactics, and professional criteria, and adapt their use to the teaching content and teaching methods of vocational college English. It is also very important for the vocational college English teachers to apply their professional knowledge, and knowledge about learning processes, to design and develop their own digital teaching materials and learning trajectory, combine different didactic methods with digital technology, digital teaching materials, and digital learning resources of vocational college English in a creative and innovative manner, so as to produce varied and adapted learning activities to guide students to have good knowledge of English and develop their language skills, as well as their cognitive and comprehensive capabilities.

3. Carefully organizing teaching implementation

Vocational college English teachers need to use digital technology to innovate teaching models and stimulate students' learning interest and potential, such as using the Internet, multimedia, cloud computing, big data and other technologies to develop and use various digital teaching resources, platforms, tools, etc., expand teaching space and time, enrich teaching forms and content, and improve teaching efficiency and quality. Based on the higher vocational college students' profiles, interests, skills, capabilities and aspirations, vocational college English teachers can recommend tailor-made content to students, monitor their progress, give feedback and adjust teaching methods based on their accumulation of knowledge and development of English language skills by using a range of digital technologies that are affordable, accessible and available. Supported by augmented reality and virtual reality, digitalization can offer students opportunities, practice and experience unseen before, and create new learning modes to make the higher vocational college students more energized and enthusiastic and improve their participation in learning. For example, mobile-based English learning apps featuring gamified elements such as"English-speaking tour guide challenges"can be utilized in vocational college English courses for students majoring in Tourism Management. Students are required to complete tasks such as describing tourist attractions in English within a time limit, answering tourists' questions correctly, and navigating through virtual tourist routes while using appropriate English phrases. The apps use augmented reality technologies to make the experience more immersive, showing lifelike images of tourist destinations. They also provide instant feedback on students' use of language, including grammar and vocabulary corrections. Teachers can track students' performances on the apps, such as their scores at different levels of the games, and use these data to adjust their in-class teaching, perhaps focusing more on areas where students are consistently making mistakes.

Blended learning, as a new and multi-dimensional teaching mode, integrates the offline teaching in the traditional classroom with online teaching of the Internet. This teaching mode combines task-based teaching with autonomous learning which helps the higher vocational college students learn before teaching, improve their critical thinking ability and comprehensive language ability, improve the quality and effectiveness of vocational college English teaching and cultivate students' core literacy in English learning, namely international communication capacity, multi-cultural communication capacity, improvement of linguistic thinking ability and development of autonomous learning capabilities. For instance, in a vocational college English course centered on business communication, teachers can create short video lectures that include real-life business scenarios, animations to explain complex business English terminologies, and voice-over translations. These videos are uploaded to online learning platforms such as Smartedu, ICVE, and Mosoteach etc. Students are requested to watch these lectures before coming to class. In the classroom, teachers then focus on facilitating group discussions, case studies, and role-playing activities related to the content of the online lectures. Through digital platforms, teachers can monitor students' viewing progress, such as how many times they re-watched a particular section and the time spent on each lecture. This blended learning mode, enabled by digital technologies, allows for more in-depth exploration of the subject matter in class and caters to students' diverse learning needs, styles and paces. Efforts should be made to achieve deep and effective teacher-student interaction and student-student interaction, such as organizing regular or irregular communication and establish effective feedback mechanisms to communicate issues and suggestions to teachers through various means (such as face-to-face, video conferencing, etc.), enhancing understanding and trust between teachers and students, and improving the quality and effectiveness of vocational college English teaching and learning.

4. Reasonably making teaching assessments

Assessment is an integral part of the teaching process; it promotes learning and confirms that students have achieved the learning outcomes of the course. By leveraging the advantages of digital technology, assessments could be made more authentic, accessible, secure, efficient, and effective in vocational college English course. In this circumstance, a variety of assessment types can be used by vocational college English teachers, including short or long answer questions, participation in discussion forums, submission of essays or case studies, reflections, as well as individual or group presentations (either live or recorded). The vocational college English teachers should bring into full play the advantages of formative assessment and summative assessment, two commonly used kinds of assessments in vocational college English course. The key advantage of formative assessment is that information is released or fed back to the English learners to help identify areas of their strengths and weaknesses and motivate them to improve their learning and future performance through hard work. Summative assessments, including examinations, play an important role in ensuring that students have factual knowledge, technical proficiency, communication, and higher order cognitive skills. Through the effective use of formative assessment and summative assessment, vocational college English teachers will give students customized tasks that are adapted to their specific needs. Students will not only learn how to master different techniques from textbooks but also from real-life experiences. Students will be guided in a risk-free environment by teachers who will encourage them to learn from their mistakes to increase and enhance their knowledge, develop their language skills and then put them into practice with the help of guided feedback. For example, in vocational college English courses, teachers can enhance formative assessment through AI-powered tools like AI Scoring System, which demonstrates exceptional efficacy in evaluating short-answer questions within business English modules, particularly for assessing grammatical accuracy and context-appropriate vocabulary usage. The AI algorithm undergoes specialized training to identify correct responses, detect common linguistic errors, and even recognize partially correct answers. For instance, when assessing students' ability to contextualize specific business English phrases, vocational college English teachers can use the platform to provide immediate feedback and real-time comprehensive analysis of syntactic structure, lexical precision, and overall language proficiency, automatically pointing out errors while providing constructive suggestions for improvement. This not only frees teachers from tedious tasks such as grading papers and scanning for errors, making suggestions, or notice when the students veer too far off topic, but also empowers the students to gain objective, timely and multifaceted insights into their overall learning performance and efficiency. Such prompt feedback mechanisms align perfectly with the principles of formative assessment by encouraging timely self-correction and targeted skills development, which are critical components for effective language acquisition in professional contexts. Additionally, with the help of digital technology, more personalized assessment system can be used by vocational college English teachers to monitor and respond to higher vocational college students' English learning. The fast feedback and adaptation to the progression of the students, coupled with direction to digital resources to remediate areas of misunderstanding, is particularly suited to formative assessment to support higher vocational college students' English learning. Furthermore, these digital platforms provide a useful means to monitor and evaluate higher vocational college students' engagement with the digital resources; recording their learning activities and progress, to facilitate interaction between students and teachers. For example, in vocational college English courses for students majoring in New Media Marketing, teachers can employ a dynamic digital portfolio evaluation app to conduct competency-based evaluations. Throughout the semester, this digital portfolio evaluation app documenting and presenting English-language projects aligned with industry demands—including crafting promotional texts for social media campaigns, producing English-subtitled video materials, and simulating cross-border e-commerce livestreaming. For summative assessment, vocational college English teachers systematically evaluate these portfolios using the platform's integrated grading features, which enable itemized scoring, nuanced written feedback, and overall performance analysis. This integrated approach not only measures linguistic accuracy but also evaluates the application of English skills in authentic working scenarios. By mirroring real-world digital communication practices, the method reinforces vocational education's emphasis on practical skill transferability while streamlining the assessment process through centralized documentation and criterion-referenced evaluation.

5. Actively building an elite teaching team

An elite teaching team is a guarantee for building high-quality vocational college English courses. Teachers with different professional backgrounds, different professional titles and different teaching experiences should be configured to form a complementary cooperation and mutually supportive relationship according to the course content and its characteristics. The teaching team should have teachers' professional ethics, such as respecting students, caring for students, and being a role model. The teaching team should have strong teaching performativity and affinity, such as being able to impart knowledge in a vivid and interesting way, stimulate students' interest, and effectively communicate with their students and establish good teacher-student relationships. Vocational college English teachers need to actively adapt to the new era, new situation and new requirements, explore the deep integration of digital technology and teacher development, and become excellent teachers with digital capabilities and literacy who can adapt to the needs of the digitalization of education in China. They should have four abilities, namely digital survival and adaptability, teaching and research capability, lifelong learning ability for professional development, and education and teaching innovation capability; achieve happy teaching, adaptive teaching and good teaching; play various roles such as organizer of students' learning activities, guide of students' growth, developer of teaching resource, innovator of teaching methods, researcher of education and teaching, and lifelong learner for professional development. To be more specific, vocational college English teachers should have corresponding digital literacy and skills, pay attention to the personalized development of English language learners; additionally, teachers must have the ability to make teaching arrangements oriented to "learner-centered", attach importance to innovation in teaching methods and changes in teaching evaluations, and be able to flexibly carry out teaching activities that integrates online and offline learning, and augmented reality and virtual reality; what's more, teachers must have the ability to build a digital learning community and be able to comprehensively use a variety of digital technologies to build a diversified, interactive, and effective learning community composed of teachers and students for mutual development through collaboration. For example, to improve the digital adaptability, competence and creativity of the vocational college English teachers, structured online professional development programs can be designed and implemented for them. For instance, recurring workshops conducted via platforms like Smartedu or ICVE could focus on Integrating Technology in English Language Teaching. A practical series titled "Digital Tools for Engaging Vocational College English Learners" might feature modules on emerging digital technologies, including AI-driven language platforms, interactive whiteboard applications, and adaptive learning software etc. During these competency-based sessions, vocational college Egnlish teachers participate in scaffolded learning training: first exploring tool functionalities through demonstrations, then applying them in simulated lesson design activities. A case study might involve training teachers to deploy intelligent writing assistances (e.g., Iwrite or Pigai) for real-time writing feedback, demonstrating how automated error detection streamlines formative assessment workflows. This immersive approach achieves dual objectives: strengthening pedagogical tech integration skills while cultivating critical digital literacies. By aligning tool mastery with classroom-ready applications such as designing AI-enhanced writing assignments or interactive vocabulary games, the program directly bridges teachers' professional development with teaching practices, ensuring the improvement of digital skills and competencies of vocational college English teachers in the digital age.

Chapter 6

Conclusion

As a compulsory course or restricted elective course for higher vocational college students of non-English majors, vocational college English course plays an important role in fostering the students' practical English-language competence, cultural awareness and intercultural communication skills, advancing their cognitive development of language learning as well as cultivating their thinking and self-expression abilities. It also helps the students develop a global mindset, expand international horizons that would lay a solid foundation for their furthering education and future career options.

Represented by cloud computing, big data, Internet of things, blockchain, artificial intelligence, virtual reality and augmented reality etc., digital technology has played a leading role in transforming and reshaping the thinking pattern, organizational structures and operational models of the human society in a fundamental and all-round manner. It empowers the construction of high-quality vocational college English courses through enriching the teaching content, updating the teaching materials, reforming the teaching modes, innovating teaching evaluations and assessments to cater to the needs of English learners in higher vocational colleges, which making the process of higher vocational college English learning more creative, experiential and inspirational.

Through the aforementioned analysis of construction of high-quality vocational college English courses empowered by digitalization, we can come to the following conclusions:

Firstly, high-quality vocational college English courses are high-level, innovative and challenging English courses. "High-level" refers to the organic integration of knowledge, ability and quality, cultivating students' comprehensive ability and advanced thinking to independently solve complex problems, and shifting from simple transfer of knowledge into a combination of transfer of knowledge, development of skills, and the shaping of character. "Innovative" means that the course content is advanced and cutting-edge, and reflect new changes in the industry and future development trends; the teaching modes are both advanced and interactive, and new ideas, new methods, and new means are used to carry out interactive teaching. "Challenging" means that academic workload and difficulty with certain degree is increased in higher vocational college English courses to add more pressure for higher vocational college students, so that the students not only need to pay close attention during class, but also conduct extra learning after school.

Secondly, based on constructivism, humanism, connectivism and mastery learning theories, construction of higher vocational college English empowered by digitalization focuses on "student-centeredness", promotes higher vocational college students to acquire English language, improve their linguistic skills, shape their core competencies and develop their learning strategies through enriching the scenario-based applications such as intelligent classroom, adaptive learning, smart diagnosis of students' learning progress, smart classroom evaluations etc., which making the process of higher vocational college English teaching and learning more creative, experiential and inspirational.

Thirdly, construction of high-quality vocational college English courses empowered by digitalization is an inevitable trend to embrace the the digital age, an essential requirement for deepening the reform of "three teachings"and an inevitable choice to improve the teaching effect of the course. But challenges and difficulties remain in building high-quality vocational college English courses empowered by digitalization such as conceptual dilemma: teachers and students' insufficient digital awareness and thinking; facility dilemma: insufficient digital infrastructure and equipment in higher vocational colleges; application dilemma: insufficient digital knowledge and skills of teachers and students.

Fourthly, in order to solve the above-mentioned problems, it is proposed that advanced concepts, reasonable principles and effective methods should be adopted to build high-quality vocational college English courses empowered by digitalization. The advanced concepts include "fostering virtue and nurturing talents", "student-centered" and "striving for excellence through hard work and comprehensive learning". The reasonable principles involve integration of ideological and political education and the vocational college English teaching, integration of industry and education and school-enterprise cooperation, making English language learning serve the practical purpose and leveraging the role of digital technology in construction of high-quality vocational college English courses. The effective methods include accurately setting teaching objectives, carefully developing teaching materials, carefully organizing teaching implementation, reasonably making teaching assessments and actively building an elite teaching team.

This study is of great significance to the construction of high-quality vocational college English courses empowered by digitalization. It can be used to improve the efficiency and effectiveness of vocational college English teaching, cultivating students' competence to apply English correctly, fluently, and appropriately in cross-cultural communication and achieve good results of English learning.

Although some progress has been made in the study of the construction of high-quality vocational college English courses empowered by digitalization, there are still certain limitations in this study that need to be further explored.

1. Regional disparities in digital infrastructure

The study's generalized approach overlooks regional variations in educational policies, economic capacity, and digital resource availability in China. Vocational colleges in economically advanced coastal regions such as the Yangtze River Delta and the Pearl River Delta often benefit from robust digital infrastructure, including 5G-enabled smart classrooms and cloud-based learning platforms. In contrast, institutions in underdeveloped areas in central and western China may rely on less-developed equipment and limited internet bandwidth, hindering access to adaptive learning tools like AI-driven grammar validators. Such disparities necessitate region-specific approaches rather than uniform solutions in construction of high-quality vocational college English courses.

2. Dynamic nature of digital technologies

Digital technologies are advancing at an astonishing pace. This study has not taken fully into account the continuous emergence of novel digital tools, platforms, and teaching-learning models. New digital-empowered language learning platforms are being developed at a rapid pace. These platforms often feature intelligent tutoring systems that can adapt to individual students' learning needs, paces and styles, provide instant feedback on language use, and even simulate real-life language scenarios through virtual reality integrations and improve students' performance without increasing their cognitive burden. The challenge for higher vocational colleges is how to keep up with the rapid development of digital technologies, particularly when it comes to taking full advantage of them to construct high-quality vocational college English courses, which provide various high-quality resources to cater to students' diverse learning needs and facilitate the teaching and learning of English in higher vocational colleges.

Further study on this subject can be conducted from the following two aspects:

Firstly, comparative case studies between higher vocational institutions in digitally advanced coastal cities and rural regions in central and western China should be conducted. Efforts should be made to analyze variables such as educational policies, economic capacity, and digital resource availability in different regions and more region-specific approaches should be further proposed to construct high-quality vocational college English courses empowered by digitalization.

Secondly, research should be continuously conducted to track the development trend of digital technologies. Efforts should be made from the following aspects involving collaboration with technology companies, participating in educational technology conferences, and conducting pilot studies on new digital tools and platforms such as setting up experimental classes to test the effectiveness of application of newly developed AI-based language learning platforms in vocational college English courses. Regular updates to the research findings based on these efforts can ensure that the proposed strategies to construct high-quality vocational college English courses empowered by digitalization remain relevant and effective in the ever-changing digital age.

Appendix Ⅰ

Criteria for Construction of High-quality Vocational College English Courses

高职公共英语金课建设标准

建设指标	建设要求
目标与学情	1. 符合新时代对技术技能人才培养新要求,落实教育部颁布的《高等职业教育专科英语课程标准(2021年版)》有关要求,紧扣学校专业人才培养方案和课程教学安排,夯实学生的英语语言基础,着力培养学生职场涉外沟通、多元文化交流、语言思维提升和自主学习完善等四项英语学科核心素养。 2. 教学目标定位准确、表述明确、相互关联,重点突出、可评可测。 3. 客观分析学生知识基础、认知能力、学习特点、专业特性等,翔实反映学生整体情况与个体差异,准确预判教学难点。
内容与策略	1. 落实课程思政要求,结合课程特点挖掘思政元素,有机融入课程教学,达到润物无声的育人效果。 2. 教学内容落实教育部颁布的《高等职业教育专科英语课程标准(2021年版)》,突出思想性、科学性、基础性、职业性和时代性,有效支撑教学目标的实现,内容组织与安排凸显职业教育类型特征,科学严谨、结构合理、逻辑清晰、衔接有序。 3. 根据《职业院校教材管理办法》等文件规定和要求选用、使用教材,建设类型丰富、内容多样的优质课程资源,满足教师教学和学习者学习需求,做到能学辅教,体现课程思政建设要求,体现行业发展的前沿技术和最新成果。 4. 教学设计科学合理,教学过程系统优化,流程环节构思得当,数智技术应用合理,方法手段设计恰当,评价考核科学有效。
实施与成效	1. 教育思想和教学理念先进,遵循学生认知规律和语言学习规律,围绕学习任务细化具体教学目标,合理把握教学进度,组织具体教学,关注重点、难点的解决。 2. 合理使用数智技术创新教学模式,案例式、混合式、探究式等多种教学方法灵活运用,教学活动开展有序,教学互动深入有效,教学气氛生动活泼,教学与管理成效显著。 3. 建立多元化学习评价体系,不断改进结果评价,强化过程评价,探索增值评价,健全综合评价。探索基于大数据的信息采集分析,全程记录和跟踪教师的教学和学生学习过程,形成教与学的正向反馈,能够针对学习反馈及时调整教学,突出学生中心,实行因材施教。 4. 课程建设过程中,不断完善课程考核评价机制,有效反思课程建设的经验与不足,教学诊断改进积极有效。

续表

建设指标	建设要求
师资团队	1. 团队结构合理，展现新时代职业院校教师良好的师德师风、教学能力和信息素养。 2. 教师课堂教学态度认真、严谨规范、语言表述清晰、亲和力强、仪态自然大方、注重教学互动、激发学生学习积极性。 3. 教师教学研究深入，学术功底扎实，教学成果积累丰富，教学改革意识强。
示范与引领	1. 在落实立德树人、文化素养提升、课程思政建设等方面有行之有效的做法，能够调动学生全面深度参与，给学生深刻的学习体验，学生对教师教学以及课程的满意度较高。 2. 在落实《高等职业教育专科英语课程标准（2021 年版）》、推进"三教"改革、运用数智技术等方面有较大的借鉴和推广价值。

Appendix Ⅱ

Case Study: Teaching Design for *Introducing Livestreaming for Agricultural Products*

Theme	Introducing Livestreaming for Agricultural Products				
Type	Reading & Speaking	Venue	Multimedia Room	Periods	2
Learning Situational Analysis	1. Students have known how to introduce agricultural products and got some basic knowledge of livestreaming for agricultural products in Chinese, but they have not got a clear idea of how to introduce livestreaimng for agricultural products in English. 2. They have known some common expressions used in introducing agricultural products, but it is difficult for them to make a presentation to introduce livestreaming for agricultural products in English.				
Teaching Objectives	Knowledge objectives 1. Grasp some words and expressions of introducing livestreaming for agricultural products; 2. Know the structure of a presentation to introduce livestreaming for agricultural products. Ability objectives 1. Be able to use the reading skill of skimming to find main ideas of the passage; 2. Be able to use the reading skill of scanning to search details of the passage; 3. Be able to make a presentation to introduce livestreaming for agricultural products.				

Continued

	Quality objectives
	1. Develop and increase awareness of the importance of livestreaming for agricultural products;
	2. Cultivate love for agricultural products, agriculture, village and farmers and build confidence in China's rural revitalization strategy and make continuous efforts to contribute to achieving China's grand goal of a strong agriculture, a beautiful countryside and well-off farmers.
Key Points	1. New words and expressions used to introduce livestreaming for agricultural products; 2. Structure of a presentation to introduce livestreaming for agricultural products; 3. Reading skills of skimming and scanning.
Difficult Points	The ability to make a presentation to introduce livestreaming for agricultural products fluently and confidently in English.
Teaching Materials & Tools	1. Textbook; 2. ICVE platform; 3. Qinglu platform; 4. WeChat official account "Suixiang English"; 5. Video.
Teaching Modes	1. Integration of theory and practice; 2. O2O teaching mode.
Teaching Methods	Task-based Teaching; Situational Teaching Approach; Activity-based Teaching; Communicative Approach; Cooperative Learning.

Teaching Process	Means
Chart for Teaching Process	Mind Map

Continued

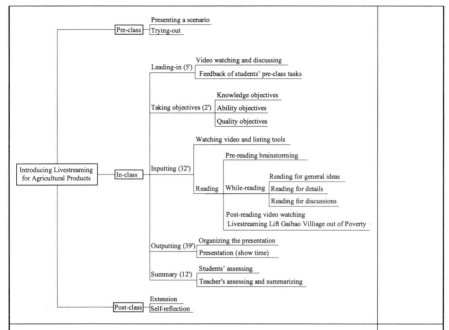

Pre-class

1. Presenting a scenario

Xiangmei Xinbao, a famous rural liverstreamer with millions of followers, is going to receive a group of exchange students from Thailand who are interested in livestreaming for agricultural products in China. Suppose you are Xiangmei Xinbao, you are going to be invited to share your rich livestreaming experience and make a presentation to introduce livestreaming for agricultural products at a formal meeting.

2. Trying-out

Xiangmei Xinbao needs to prepare for the presentation. Imagine you are Xiangmei Xinbao, how will you arrange the content and stucture of the presentation.

Please discuss with your team members about how to make a presentation to introduce livestreaming for agricultural products

Autonomous

Learning

Continued

according to the related materials on ICVE platform and "Suixiang" Wechat official account and then send your videos to the platform.	Situational Teaching Approach

In-class

Step I Leading-in (5 minutes)

1. Video watching and discussing

Ask students to watch a clip of video of Xiangmei Xinbao.

Discussing: What has she done? Can you say something about her?

Words and Expressions for References		
rural livestreamer followers ……	vocational school graduate migrant worker return to hometown ……	sell local farm produce raise income lift out of poverty ……

Communicative Approach

Suggested answer: She is a famous rural liverstreamer with millions of followers...

2. Feedback of students' pre-class tasks.

Step Ⅱ Taking objectives (2 minutes)

1. Knowledge objectives

Grasp some words and expressions of introducing livestreaming for agricultural products;

Know the structure of a presentation to introduce livestreaming for agricultural products.

2. Ability objectives

Be able to use the reading skill of skimming to find main ideas of the passage;

Be able to use the reading skill of scanning to search details of the passage;

Be able to make a presentation to introduce livestreaming for agricultural products.

Tips:
Cultivate students' love for agricultural products, agriculture, village and farmers

Continued

3. Quality objectives Develop and increase awareness of the importance of livestreaming for agricultural products; Cultivate love for agricultural products, agriculture, village and farmers and build confidence on China's rural revitalization strategy and make continuous efforts to contribute to achieving China's grand goal of a strong agriculture, a beautiful countryside and well-off farmers. **Step III Inputting (32 minutes)** 1. Watching video and listing tools Directions: Watch a short video and discuss the tools needed for live streaming for agricultural products. Question: What are the tools needed for livestreaming for agricultrual products? When watching the video, please list the tools needed for livestreaming for agricultrual products. Suggested answers: a computer or a cellphone with access to the Internet and a livestream platform or application for broadcasting. 2. Reading ✦ Pre-reading Question: Besides tools needed for livestreaming for agricultrual products, what aspects can be included in introducing livestreaming for farm produce? Suggested answers: advantages, benefits, suggestions or tips for livestreaming for farm produce. ✦ While-reading: (1) Reading for general ideas Students skim the passage *Live-stream Marketing: A Rural Rags-*	 Inquiry Learning Task-based

Continued

to-riches Story within stipulated time to get a general idea of the passage and try to answer the following question: What does the title "Live-stream Marketing: A Rural Rags-to-Riches Story" mean? Suggested answer: Rags-to-riches: from poor to rich. Live-stream marketing is currently an effective marketing channel for farmers to sell their farm products to consumers across the country and around the world. It helps farmers raise their income and lift themselves out of poverty. (2) Reading for details Students scan the passage within stipulated time to finish the following tasks in Qinglu platform. (Platform will give feedback and give marks) Directions: Please choose the best answer from the four choices marked A, B, C and D. Q1: Which of the following statements is incorrect according to the passage? (　　　) A. China is a big agricultural country. B. China is lack of agricultural resources. C. China has a longstanding tradition of intensive cultivation. D. China has a huge rural population. Q2: High quality agricultrual products can now travel to consumers nationwide and worldwide at　(　　　)　than before. A. at higher logistics costs and higher speeds B. at lower logistics costs and lower speeds C. at lower logistics costs and higher speeds D. at higher logistics costs and lower speeds	Teaching Tips: Develop and increase students' awareness of the importance of livestreaming for agricultural products Brainstorming Task-based Teaching

Continued

Q3: With the expansion of the industrial chain, many relevant businesses in and around China's more isolated villages can "get a free ride". Which of the following businesses is not mentioned in the passage?   (   )

A. Logistics

B. Packaging

C. The deep processing of agricultrual products

D. Insurance

Q4: E-commerce live-streaming is doing pretty well nowadays, but agricultrual products only accounts for a small share, mainly due to   (   ) .

A. the lack of funds in rural areas

B. the lack of experienced hosts and infrastructure in rural areas

C. the lack of infrastructure in rural areas

D. the lack of support from governments

Q5: The key to growing live-stream marketing for agricultrual products is   (   ) .

A. to meet consumers' demands

B. to develop high-quality products

C. to consider buyers' preference

D. to increase investment in infrastructure in rural areas

(3) Reading for discussion

Directions: Students read the passage for the third time and discuss the following 3 questions within their groups and try to answer the questions.

(Group discussion and choose one group member to answer the questions.)

Continued

Q1: What were the problems of agricultrual products in remote regions in China?

Suggested answers:

For many years, premium agricultural products were unable to sell in remote regions due to a lack of efficient marketing channels, preventing them from accessing a wider market.

Q2: What are the advantages of livestreaming for agricultrual products?

Suggested answers:

Firstly, high quality agricultrual products can now travel to consumers nationwide and worldwide at lower logistics costs and higher speeds, than before.

Secondly, live-stream marketing may appeal to young migrant workers and convince them to return home in the countryside. Once back, they can introduce more digitally advanced approaches to agricultural management.

Thirdly, live-stream marketing creates a lot of direct and indirect job opportunities and creates an effective strategy for income generation.

Q3: What are the suggestions for live streaming for agricultrual products?

Suggested answers:

First of all, the key to grow live-stream marketing for agricultrual products is to meet consumers' demands.

In addition, live-stream marketing can be combined with the expansion of smart agriculture and smart villages.

Last but not least, supporting government policies and guidance should follow up and further standardize live-stream marketing.

Continued

	Tips:
♨ Post-reading: Video watching Share the story *Live Streaming Lift Gaibao Villiage out of Poverty* to help students have a better understanding of the passage *Live-stream Marketing: A Rural Rags-to-Riches Story.* **Step Ⅳ Outputting (39 minutes)** 1. Organizing the presentation Make an outline of the presentation to introduce livestreaming for agricultrual products by finishing the following structure with the information that students have got in "Inputting". A presentation to introduce livestreaming for agricultrual products	Cultivate students' love for agricultural products, agriculture, village and farmers and build students' confidence in China's rural revitalization strategy.

Assignments: please finish the following structure of a presentation		
Starter …it is a great honour for me to…livestreaming for agricultural products…l will introduce it from the following 3 aspects:		
Tools tools are very important… …a computer or a cellphone …a live stream platform or application…	Advantages there are mainly… advantages… firstly… secondly… thirdly…	Suggestions the major suggestions for …are…as follows: first of all in addition… last but not least…
Ending …thank you so much for your listening.		

2. Presentation (Show time)

Instruct students to work in groups to make a presentation to introduce livestreaming for agricultrual products. Each group could select one group member to give a presentation to introduce livestreaming for agricultrual products. Students are required to pay attentions to their pronunciation and intonation, fluency, structure, body languages and facial expressions.

Step Ⅴ Summary (12 minutes)

1. Students' assessing

(1) Each student is required to cast a vote for the group which

Cooperative

Learning

Continued

he/she prefers except his/her own group.

(2) Each student is required to complete a questionnaire on the Qinglu platform for each group and provide feedback on their pronunciation and intonation, fluency, structrue, body languages and facial expressions.

2. Teacher's assessing and summarizing

Assessing Points
pronunciation and intonation,fluency,body languages and facial expressions
structure of a presentation to introduce livestreaming for agricultural products

Structure of a Presentation to Introduce Livestreaming for Agricultural Products
- Starter
- Body — Tools / Advantages / Suggestions
- Ending

Collaborative Assessment

Post-class

1. Extension

(1) Ask students to read more materials about introducing livestreaming for agricultrual products on Wechat official account "Suixiang English".

(2) Ask students to work in groups to make a video to make a presentation to introduce livestreaming for agricultrual products and upload the video to ICVE platform.

(3) Students assess each other's presentation videos on the platform.

(4) Teacher assesses each group's presentation video on the platform.

Autonomous Learning

Continued

2. Self-reflection

Ask students to go through the evaluation list and compare their work

with others.

Self-reflection

Rate your progress in this section	D	M	P	F
I master useful words and expressions of introducing livestreaming for agricultural products.	☐	☐	☐	☐
I know the structure of a presentation to introduce livestreaming for agricultural products.	☐	☐	☐	☐
I have developed my reading skills of skimming and scanning.	☐	☐	☐	☐
I can make a presentation to introduce livestreaming for agricultural products fluently and confidently.	☐	☐	☐	☐
I have the awareness of the importance of livestreaming for agricultural products.	☐	☐	☐	☐
I love agricultural products,agriculture,village and farmers and have confidence in China's rural revitalization strategy	☐	☐	☐	☐

Blackboard design

教学后记：

本堂课课型为"读说课"，讲授的内容为直播助农我来"享"，反思教学实施

成效与改进措施如下：

1. 成效反思

（1）创设职场情境，激发学习的积极性：课前创设情境，设计真实交际场景，

引导学生代入职场角色——直播助农网红主播"湘妹心宝"，尝试用英语分享其

丰富的直播助农经验，用英文向来自泰国的交换生介绍直播助农的产出任务，让

学生认识产出任务的交际价值和自身不足，激发学生的学习积极性。

（2）强调产出导向，坚持学以致用：课中强调产出导向，以激发学生学习主动

性的"交际活动"为切入点，灵活使用情境、任务、合作学习等多种教学方法，

为学生提供丰富的素材输入，同时根据学生的"最近发展区"特点搭建"脚手架"，

在语言表达、语篇结构、语用策略以及文化交际方面提供指导，逐步引导学生完

成最终用英语介绍直播助农的产出任务，从而培养学生职场涉外沟通、多元文化

交流、语言思维提升和自主学习完善等核心素养。

（3）巧妙融入思政，注重品德培养：通过让学生观看湘妹心宝、新农具&新农

活、盖宝村直播助农等视频，让学生加深对农村经济、直播助农、脱贫攻坚、乡

村振兴的认同感，强化其为新时代"三农"工作和乡村振兴贡献一份力量的责任

和担当，充分发挥其电子商务专业的优势，积极投入到直播助农实践中，努力做

热心知农品、衷心爱农业、全心助农人、创新务农活的新时代"新农人"。

Continued

2. 改进措施

由于部分学生积累的词汇量有限，在阅读文本的过程中速度较慢、效率不高，阅读热情不高。因此，教师需充分利用教学平台，以线上与线下相结合的方式给学生个性化辅导，引导学生养成良好的阅读习惯，通过丰富的阅读实践来掌握精读、略读、速读、跳读等阅读方法，提高学生的阅读能力。

Bibliography

[1] 国务院. 国务院关于印发国家职业教育改革实施方案的通知 [EB/OL].（2019-02-13）[2024-07-08]. https://www.gov.cn/zhengce/ zhengceku/2019-02/13/content_5365341.htm.

[2] 中华人民共和国职业教育法[EB/OL].（2022-4-21）[2024-07-08]. http://www.xinhuanet.com/2022-04/21/c_1128579359.htm.

[3] 教育部. 教育部办公厅关于印发高等职业教育专科英语，信息技术 课程标准（2021 年版）的通知[EB/OL].（2021-04-09）[2024-07-08]. http://www.moe.gov.cn/srcsite/A07/moe_737/s3876_qt/202104/t2021 0409_525482.html.

[4] 国务院. 中共中央，国务院印发《中国教育现代化 2035》[EB/OL]. （2019-02-23）[2024-07-08]. https://www.gov.cn/zhengce/2019-02/23 /content_5367987.htm.

[5] 国务院. 国务院关于印发新一代人工智能发展规划的通知[EB/O L].（2017-07-20）[2024-07-08]. https://www.gov.cn/zhengce/ cont ent/2017-07/20/content_5211996.htm.

[6] 教育部. 教育部关于印发《教育信息化 2.0 行动计划》的通知[EB/O L].（2018-04-25）[2024-07-08]. http://www.moe.gov.cn/srcsite/ A1 6/ s3342/201804/t20180425_334188.html.

[7] HSIEH Y. J., WU Y. J. Entrepreneurship through the platform strategy in the digital era: insights and research opportunities[J]. Computers in human behavior, 2019(05): 315-323.

[8] KOZINETS R. V., FERREIRA D. A., CHIMENTI P. How do platforms empower consumers? Insights from the affordances and constraints of reclame aqui[J]. Journal of consumer research, 2021, 48(03): 428-455.

[9] YE L., YANG H. From digital divide to social inclusion: a tale of mobile platform empowerment in rural areas[J]. Sustainability, 2020, 12(06): 2424.

[10] SPREITZER G. M. Psychological empowerment in the workplace: Dimensions, measurement, and validation[J]. Academy of management journal, 1995, 38(05): 1442-1465.

[11] WHITMORE E. Participation, empowerment and welfare[J]. Canadian review of social policy, 1988(22): 51-60.

[12] KEIFFER C. Citizen empowerment: a developmental perspective[J]. Prevention in human services, 1984, 3(16):9-35.

[13] WALLERSTEIN N. Powerlessness, empowerment and health: Implications for health promotion programs[J]. American journal of health promotion, 1992, 6(3):197-205.

[14] RAPPAPORT J. Terms of empowerment/exemplars of prevention: Toward a theory for community psychology[J]. American journal of community psychology, 1987, 15(2):121-148.

[15] PRESBY J., WANDERSMAN A., FLORIN P., RICH R., CHAVIS D. Benefits, costs, incentive management and particpation in voluntary organizations: A means to understanding and promoting empowerment[J]. American journal of community psychology, 1990, 18(1): 117-148.

[16] LABONTE R. Community empowerment: the need for political analysis[J]. Canadian journal of public health, 1989, 80(2):87-88.

[17] HYMESD H. On communicative competence[C]. Harmonsworth: Penguin, 1972.

[18] Hutchinson T., Waters A. English for specific purposes: a learning-centred approach[M]. Cambridge: Cambridge University Press, 1987.

[19] HARRISA, ET AL. Improving schools in challenging contexts: exploring the possible[J]. School effectiveness and school improvement，2006,17(04): 409-424.

[20] ELIZABETH PLATT. The vocational classroom: a great place to learn english[R]. English for specific purposes: a learning-centred approach. Cambridge University Press, 1987.

[21] CARTER AMANDA G., CREEDY DEBRA K., SIDEBOTHAM MARY. Efficacy of teaching methods used to develop critical thinking in nursing and midwifery undergraduate students: A systematic review of the literature[J]. Nurse education today. 2016(40): 209-218.

[22] SAUL MCLEOD. Constructivism Learning Theory & Philosophy of Education[EB/OL]. (2024-2-01). https://www.simplypsychology.org/constructivism.html.

[23] ARENDS R. I. Resource handbook. Learning to teach[M]. 4th ed. Boston, MA: McGraw-Hill, 1998.

[24] ELLIOTT S. N., KRATOCHWILL T. R., LITTLEFIELD COOK J., TRAVERS J. Educational psychology: effective teaching, effective learning [M]. 3rd ed. Boston, MA: McGraw-Hill College, 2000.

[25] GUSKEY T. R. Lessons of mastery learning[J]. Educational Leadership: interventions that work, 2010, 68(2): 52-57.

[26] ARISTIZÚBAL J. Using learning analytics to improve students' reading skills: a case study in an american international school with English as an Addition Language (EAL) students[J]. GiST education and learning research journal, 2018(17):193-214.

[27] WILLIAM F. HOLLIS. Humanistic learning theory and instructional technology: is reconciliation possible?[J]. Educational technology, 1991, 31(11): 49-53.

[28] MD. AFROZ ALAM. Connectivism learning theory and connectivist approach in teaching and learning: a review of literature[J]. Bhartiyam international journal of education & research, 2023,12(2):1-15.

[29] BOULTON A., J. THOMAS. In input, process and product: developments in teaching and language corpora[M]. Bro: Masaryk

University Press, 2012.

[30] JEON J. Chatbot-assisted dynamic assessment (CA-DA) for L2 vocaburary learning and diagnosis[J]. Computer assisted language learning, 2021(7): 1338-1364.

[31] KHALIFA A., KATO T., S. YAMAMOTO. Learning effect of implicit learning in joining-in-type robot-assisted language learning system[J]. Inernational joural of emerging teehnologies in learning, 2019(2): 105-123.

[32] LEE D., KIM H. H., S. H. SUNG, Development research on an Al English learning support system to faclitute learner-generated-context-based learning[J]. Educational technology research and deelopmemt, 2023(2): 629-666.

[33] POKRIVCAKOVA S. Preparing teachers for the application of AI-powered technologies in foreign language education[J]. Journal of language and cultural education, 2019(3): 135-153.

[34] TAFAZOLI D., MARIA, E. G., C. A. H. ABRIL. Intelligent language tutoring system: integrating intelligent computer-assisted language learning into language education[J]. International journal of information and communication technology education，2019(3): 60-74.

[35] BOYCKAERT M. Current perspectives on teachers as materials developers: why, what, and how?[J]. RELC Joumal, 2019(3):439-456.

[36] CAFABANTES L., A. PARAN. "I preferred to take another activity from the textbook": an activity-theoretical study of learning to design language teaching materials[J]. The modern language journal, 2022(4): 659-674.

[37] FRESTONE A. R., CRUZ R. A., J. E. RODL. Teacher study groups: an integrative literature synthesis[J]. Review of educational research, 2020(5):675-709.

[38] SIMS S. H. FLETCHER WOOD. Identifying the characteristics of

effective teacher professional development: a critical review [J]. School effectiveness and school improvement, 2021 (1): 47-63.

[39] 陈海贝，卓翔芝. 数字赋能研究综述[J]. 图书馆论坛，2019(6): 53-60, 132.

[40] 胡春辉. 物流企业的数字化赋能影响因素研究[D]. 合肥: 安徽大学，2020.

[41] 李卓君. 数字化赋能职业教育"1+X"证书制度的价值共创研究[J]. 齐齐哈尔大学学报（哲学社会科学版），2021(01): 175-179.

[42] 李晓娟，王屹. 技术赋能：职业院校教师数字素养的要义，挑战及提升[J]. 中国职业技术教育，2021(23): 31-37, 45.

[43] 张青山. 数字化赋能职业教育高质量发展的思考[J]. 中国职业技术教育，2022(11): 59-63.

[44] 贺书霞，孙超，冀涛. 数智化赋能职业教育产教融合探索[J]. 教育与职业，2024(03): 23-28.

[45] 董亚楠. 数字化背景下高职院校英语教师职业能力提升路径探究[J]. 开封大学学报，2021, 35(04): 58-59.

[46] 高冲，项成东. 数字赋能高职英语教学高质量发展实践研究[J]. 天津职业院校联合学报，2023, 25(03): 42-49.

[47] 张越. 高职院校职业英语教学的现状及对策[J]. 海外英语，2013(20): 76-77.

[48] 马琼，宋正富. 高职英语课程教学探索[J]. 中国高等教育，2021 (10): 59-61.

[49] 朱莹，刘真平. 从"围观"到"体验"：高职英语课堂变革的实践取向[J]. 教育与职业，2020 (21): 100-103.

[50] 滕春燕. "一带一路"背景下高职英语教师国际化发展的机遇，问题与出路[J]. 教育与职业，2020 (11): 80-86.

[51] 易红波. 需求分析视角下高职公共英语教学模式研究[J]. 中国高校科技，2023 (12): 103.

[52] 陈湘云. 核心素养体系下的大学英语课堂教学探索[J]. 辽宁科技学

院学报，2017, 19 (01): 52-54+68.

[53] 吴岩. 建设中国"金课"[J]. 中国大学教学，2018(12): 4-9.

[54] 李志义. "水课"与"金课"之我见[J]. 中国大学教学，2018 (12): 24-29.

[55] 邓忠波. 大学课程中"水课"现象审视与"金课"建设进路[J]. 中国电化教育，2020 (04): 68-74.

[56] 余廷忠，贺道德，黄正鹏，胡如会，王艳. 应用型大学计算机基础一流课程的建设及教学[J]. 贵州工程应用技术学院学报，2020, 38 (03): 124-129.

[57] 蒋雯，邓鑫洋，耿杰. "双一流"背景下研究生《智能信息处理与融合技术》课程建设探索[J]. 黑龙江教育（高教研究与评估），2020 (11): 75-76.

[58] 刘文锴. 聚力特色"金课"建设办好新时代行业特色高水平本科教育[J]. 中国高等教育，2020 (18): 20-22.

[59] 朱善元，胡新岗，朱明苑. 高职数字化教学"金课"的内涵特征，价值意蕴及建设路径[J]. 教育与职业，2023 (04): 89-94.

[60] 胡万山，周海涛. 提升高校教师"金课"建设效能[J]. 现代大学教育，2019 (06): 31-35.

[61] 谢幼如，黄瑜玲，黎佳，赖慧语，邱艺. 融合创新，有效提升"金课"建设质量[J]. 中国电化教育，2019 (11): 9-16.

[62] 薄蓉蓉，冷明祥. 高校"金课"建设的基本认知，现实困境与实践路径[J]. 黑龙江高教研究，2019, 37 (08): 141-144.

[63] 兰水. 高职院校思政"金课"建设：现实困境与基本路径[J]. 鄂州大学学报，2023, 30 (03): 16-19.

[64] 邓莉，彭正梅. 迈向2030年的课程变革：以美国和芬兰为例[J]. 湖南师范大学教育科学学报，2018, 17 (01): 99-108.

[65] 薛瑞丽，李华，李海霞，汪月霞. 农林院校植物生理学课程教学如何去"水"存"金"[J]. 教育现代化，2019, 6 (57): 212-213.

[66] 黄浩. 数字化何以赋能教师专业发展[N]. 中国教师报，2024-05-22（13）.

[67] 肖迎春. 数字化赋能高等教育高质量发展[N]. 中国教育报，2024-03-25（4）.

[68] 李帆，董鲁，皖龙. 智能时代，教育的"变局"与"新机"——"人工智能赋能教育"系列之一[N]. 中国教育报，2024-03-01（4）.

[69] 易祯，吴美玉. 从"混合"到"融合"：线上线下融合式教学设计研究[J]. 中国教育信息化，2023，29(11): 84-96.

[70] 王繁，刘永强，周天华. 人工智能引领高等教育数字化创新发展[J]. 中国高等教育，2024 (Z1)：9-12.

[71] 王小飒. 探索数字化赋能高校英语教学路径[EB/OL].（2023-05-31）. https://reader.gmw.cn/2023-05/31/content_36600482.htm.

[72] 李杰. 探索高校英语教学数字化转型新路径[N]. 新华日报，2024-04-19（14）.

[73] 张敬源，赵红艳. 数字化转型背景下的大学英语教学创新路径[J]. 外语学刊，2024 (02): 84-91.

[74] 张鹏，杨聚鹏，秦莉红. 数字化转型赋能高职教学高质量发展的意涵，逻辑与进路[J]. 教育与职业，2024 (09): 82-89.

[75] 颜翔，吴庆华. AIGC 赋能高职院校教学数字化转型探索[J]. 职业教育研究，2024 (05): 26-31.

[76] 何曼. 数字化赋能建构大规模个性化英语教学范式[J]. 在线学习，2024 (Z1)：50-53, 92.

[77] 戴馨，欧俐岑. 人工智能视域下职业教育在线金课构建研究[J]. 鄂州大学学报，2022, 29 (05)：87-89.

[78] 杨勇，林旭. "人工智能＋教育"视域下职业教育"金课"建设[J]. 中国职业技术教育，2019 (23)：69-74.

[79] 刘光洁，朱金龙. "金课"概念下的数字化资源建设[J]. 计算机教育，2019 (11)：38-41.

[80] 拾以超，王碧君. 数据赋能 着力打造"数字化"课程[N]. 中国教育报，2023-06-19（8）.

[81] 王逸铭. 智慧教育助力大学生英语自主学习[N]. 中国教育报，2023-

06-19（8）.

[82] 王海涛. 数字化如何赋能课程教学改革[N]. 中国教育报，2023-12-11（9）.

[83] 李金雪，吴金航. 数字化赋能职业院校高质量教学：表征样态与实现路径[J]. 职业教育研究，2024（06）：84-90.

[84] 毛海舟. 数字时代"三教"改革赋能高职教育高质量发展研究[J]. 中国成人教育，2023（23）：19-22.

[85] 王丽君. 数字化转型背景下高职院校职业场景应用的教学转化研究[J]. 中国职业技术教育，2023（07）：41-47,55.

[86] 张柏柯，易明. 数字技术赋能课程改革与教学模式创新研究——以《英语写作》课程为例[J]. 中国电化教育，2023（12）：106-112,120.

[87] 吴坚豪，周婉婷，曹超. 生成式人工智能技术赋能口语教学的实证研究[J]. 中国电化教育，2024（04）：105-111.

[88] 郑春萍，于淼，郭智妍. 人工智能在语言教学中的应用研究：回顾与展望[J]. 外语教学，2024,45（01）:59-68.

[89] 包宗鑫. 智慧教育视角下大学英语教学改革创新途径研究[J]. 赤峰学院学报（汉文哲学社会科学版），2023,44（10）:110-113.

[90] 崔媛. 基于人工智能技术的高职英语生态教学实践[J]. 湖南教育（C版），2023（09）：57-59.

[91] 卢静. 数字化时代大学英语教学改革的机遇，挑战与路径[J]. 山东农业工程学院学报，2023,40（08）：125-128.

[92] 方旭，许磊. 人工智能时代大学生英语写作自动批改工具使用行为意向研究[J]. 外语教育研究，2023,11（03）：34-40.

[93] 王东旭. 中职英语数字化教学资源使用困境与区块链技术赋能脱困之策[D]. 湘潭：湖南科技大学，2023.

[94] 焦建利，陈婷. 大型语言模型赋能英语教学：四个场景[J]. 外语电化教学，2023（02）：12-17,106.

[95] 曾立英，金心怡，陈艺宣. 人工智能支持的英语图文推理及教学应用[J]. 西安外国语大学学报，2023,31（01）：59-65.

[96] 郑佩芸. 基于深度知识追踪的大学英语智适应学习系统构建初探[J]. 外语电化教学, 2023 (01): 53-56, 112.

[97] 刘应亮, 刘胜蓝, 杨进才. 社会文化活动理论视域下人机协同教学及应用探索——以 iWrite 协同英语写作教学为例[J]. 中国电化教育, 2022 (11): 108-116.

[98] 梁君英, 向明友, 闵尚超, 陈向京, 周杰. 科教融合 东西联动——大学英语课程虚拟教研室建设理念与路径[J]. 外语界, 2022 (04): 2-7.

[99] 林翔. "互联网＋"背景下英语"金课"建设教学模式创新与实践[J]. 鄂州大学学报, 2024, 31 (02): 83-84.

[100] 董晓烨, 杨甦祺. 近四年国内高校英语金课研究综述 (2019—2022)[J]. 邵阳学院学报 (社会科学版), 2024, 23 (01): 100-106.

[101] 袁平华, 谭涛. 基于 CBI 的线上线下"金课"模式对学生英语学习动机及自主学习能力的影响研究[J]. 外语与翻译, 2023, 30 (04): 56-61, 98.

[102] 陈婉颖. 高校英语混合式"金课"建设实践研究[J]. 吉林农业科技学院学报, 2023, 32 (06): 100-104.

[103] 杨宇. 智慧教学背景下高职英语金课构建[J]. 鄂州大学学报, 2023, 30 (05): 85-86.

[104] 姬京彤. 高校英语线上线下混合式"金课"建设[J]. 山西财经大学学报, 2023, 45 (S1): 193-195.

[105] 却俊. 基于"金课"标准的高校英语混合式教学课程建设研究[J]. 长春大学学报, 2022, 32 (12): 82-84, 94.

[106] 袁平华, 谭涛, 龚沁怡. 基于学科内容的线上线下"金课"教学模式对大学生英语应用能力和思辨能力影响研究[J]. 外语与翻译, 2022, 29 (04): 73-79, 98.

[107] 蔡满园. "课程思政"视域下大学英语金课的创意理性及实践路向[J]. 外语电化教学, 2022 (01): 3-7, 101.

[108] 杨舒琳, 李瑞. 数字化时代大学英语课堂教学质量评估模型构建

研究[J]. 西安外国语大学学报，2021, 29 (04): 78-81.

[109] 张建利. 基于"金课"标准的高校英语读写课堂教学设计研究[J]. 长春大学学报，2021 , 31 (02): 77-80.

[110] 张丹. 大学英语混合式金课的构建与实践研究[J]. 外语电化教学，2021 (01): 71-77, 91, 12.

[111] 刘芳. "三教"改革背景下高职院校基础英语金课建设路径探究[J]. 鄂州大学学报，2021, 28 (01): 39-41.

[112] 郭欣. 线上＋线下混合教育模式下英语"金课"教学的研究[J]. 长春大学学报，2020, 30 (12): 102-104+108.

[113] 屈江丽，周爽. "互联网＋"多模态技术辅助下英语"金课"的设计与启示[J]. 西安外国语大学学报，2020, 28 (04): 60-64.

[114] 李芳媛，杨蓉. 大学英语"金课"建设质量评估体系模型构建[J]. 外语界，2020 (04): 71-79.

[115] 魏晓冰. 基于 BOPPPS 教学模型的大学英语"金课"探索[J]. 长春工程学院学报（社会科学版），2020, 21 (01): 149-152.

[116] 陈冬纯，武敏. 试论大学英语"金课"的质量标准与评估体系[J]. 外语电化教学，2019 (05): 27-32.

[117] 蔡基刚. 公共英语"金课"标准——为学生专业学习和科研创新插上语言翅膀[J]. 浙江外国语学院学报，2019 (03): 1-7.

[118] 陈凌. 人工智能推动高校英语教师角色重构[N]. 新华日报，2024-04-12（14）.

[119] 王立非，任杰. 商务英语"金课"标准的"六性"与"六度"[J]. 浙江外国语学院学报，2019 (03): 13-18.

[120] 郑春萍，许玲玉，高梦雅，卢志鸿，程倩倩，杨紫彤. 虚拟现实技术应用于语言教学的系统性文献综述（2009—2018）[J]. 外语电化教学，2019 (04): 39-47.

[121] 王建华，李润美. "元宇宙"视域下基于虚拟现实技术的语言教学研究[J]. 外语电化教学，2022 (01): 40-47, 107.

[122] 胡加圣，戚亚娟. ChatGPT 时代的中国外语教育：求变与应变[J]. 外

语电化教学，2023 (01): 3-6, 105.

[123] 徐莉，梁震，杨丽乐. 人工智能＋教育融合的困境与出路——复杂系统科学视角[J]. 中国电化教育, 2021(5): 78-86.

[124] 岳曼曼，刘正光. 混合式教学契合外语课程思政：理念与路径[J]. 外语教学，2020(6): 15-19.

[125] 张文忠，翟宇，张晨. 外语教学实践问题调查[J]. 外语与外语教学，2021(1): 46-56.

Acknowledgments

I would like to take this chance to express my heartfelt thanks to everyone who has made efforts and offered support for the research, writing, and publishing of the book. I am very grateful to all the honorable professors who have helped me and benefited me a lot during my four years of undergraduate study in School of Foreign Languages, Jiangxi University of Finance and Economics and three years of post-graduate study in School of Foreign Languages, Central South University. Their optimistic attitude, profound knowledge, broad vision, deep insight as well as their logical, critical and creative thinking have had a remarkable impact on me. Their important guidance, great encouragement, invaluable suggestions, constructive comments contribute to my career development as an English teacher in higher vocational colleges.

Then, I want to express my deep and sincere gratitude to my colleagues and friends who have carefully read and critiqued this book. Their friendly help and valuable comments helped me improve the clarity and readability of this book.

A special note of thanks also goes to the editors in the Southwest Jiaotong University Press whose meticulous work and full support has been invaluable.

Finally, I also wish to extend my heartfelt thanks to my family for their love and ever-lasting support.